34

W9-BXP-020

BLUE
VS.
BLACK

BLUE VS. BLACK

Let's End the Conflict Between Cops and Minorities

John L. Burris
with Catherine Whitney

ST. MARTIN'S PRESS   NEW YORK

BLUE VS. BLACK: LET'S END THE CONFLICT BETWEEN COPS AND MINORITIES. Copyright © 1999 by John L. Burris and Catherine Whitney. All rights reserved. Printed in the United States of America. No part of this book may be used or reproduced in any manner whatsoever without written permission except in the case of brief quotations embodied in critical articles or reviews. For information, address St. Martin's Press, 175 Fifth Avenue, New York, N.Y. 10010.

Designed by Kathryn Parise

Photographs by Paul Whitney

Library of Congress Cataloging-in-Publication Data
Burris, John L.
    Blue vs. black: let's end the conflict between cops and
minorities / John L. Burris; with Catherine Whitney.
        p.   cm.
    Includes bibliographical references.
    ISBN 0-312-20392-6
    1. Police brutality—United States—Case studies.
 2. Discrimination in law enforcement—United States—Case studies.
 3. Afro-Americans—Civil rights—United States.   4. Police
brutality—United States—Prevention.   5. Discrimination in law
enforcement—United States—Prevention.   I. Whitney, Catherine.
 II. Title
 HV8141.B85   1999
 363.2'32—dc21   99-22180
                                                          CIP

First Edition: September 1999

10   9   8   7   6   5   4   3   2   1

*For all those who have felt
the sting of police abuse,
without remedy or justice.
For the invisible faces, the
unheard voices, the stolen lives.*

CONTENTS

ACKNOWLEDGMENTS   ix
FOREWORD: A Hope of Healing   1
CHAPTER 1:   A Man Who Cried   5
CHAPTER 2:   Blacks and Cops in Conflict   15
CHAPTER 3:   The Measure of a Man   27
CHAPTER 4:   What Children See   41
CHAPTER 5:   The Fox in the Henhouse   61
CHAPTER 6:   Walking While Black   81
CHAPTER 7:   The Continuum   107
CHAPTER 8:   The Black Sea   123
CHAPTER 9:   Ain't I a Woman?   141
CHAPTER 10:   A Failure to Communicate   155
CHAPTER 11:   Skin So Blue   169
CHAPTER 12:   The Partnership   187
CHAPTER 13:   The Making of a Good Cop   203
CHAPTER 14:   A Blueprint for Police Reform   213
AFTERWORD: As the Twig Is Bent . . .   223
NOTES   227
INDEX   235

ACKNOWLEDGMENTS

I have been blessed at every point in my life to be supported by individuals who have enabled me to be more and to do more than I ever thought possible. My contribution to the struggle, as reflected in this book, is a fitting legacy for my parents, DeWitt and Imogene Burris, who taught me that individuals can make a difference. This is the result of their hard work and love, as well as the nurturing and support my aunts and uncles provided. During my youth they gave me vision when I had no view beyond my own town.

I am indebted to Ramona Tascoe, who has never hesitated to urge me on, with a sharp mind and a passion for justice that is unequaled. I am blessed with a wonderful group of siblings. My sisters, Faye, Loretta (now deceased), and Bobbie, and my brothers, Clint and Ron, have always been a source of pride and inspiration. My children, Damon, Monique, Justin, Courtney, and Jonathan, and my nieces and nephews, are the living testimony of the importance of my work. The recent arrival of my first granddaughter, Maya Simone, born to Damon and his wife Tracy, further strengthens my commitment to a future that will not be marred by racism.

Clinton White, retired justice of the California appellate court, was my inspiration in the 1960s and 1970s as the premier criminal lawyer in the area. He showed me the nobility of fighting for justice. Henry Ramsey, my professor in law school, walked with me through troubled waters. I continue to be grateful for the friendship of Henry and his wife, Eleanor. I deeply appreciate the friendship of Dr. George Woods, my intellectual soul mate, and the insights that have emerged from our many years of dialogue. Richard Freeman has been a constant source of friendship and support.

I am thankful to the many people who have stood beside me and helped me along the way. Robert Harris, now a lawyer, was my first friend when I left home. He encouraged me to go to law school, and we shared many dreams and secrets. My younger cousin, Reginald Terrell, has provided stability and vision in my office. Judge Willie Mae Whiting was my mentor in Chicago. She taught me the fundamentals of trial practice and how to survive in the big city. I am grateful to my first law partners, Elihu Harris and Dave Alexander, with whom I shared so much, and who gave me the opportunity to follow my heart and my destiny. Johnnie L. Cochran was an inspiration and a friend to me long before he became famous, and he continues to be one of my most valuable sounding boards. Special thanks to Paul Rein who has been a supportive colleague. Paul and his wife, Brenda, have been especially good friends to me.

I am continually empowered by, and indebted to, my colleagues in police misconduct work: Charles Bonner, Pamela Price, James Chanin, Ted Harris, Matthew Kumin, Steven Yourke, Andrew Schwartz, Stephen Collier, Oliver Jones, and the Bay Area Police Watch. I am also especially grateful to Milton Grimes, an outstanding criminal lawyer who brought me into the Rodney King civil case, and to Federico Sayre, an excellent plaintiff's lawyer whose grasp of medical issues made an important difference in the King case. I also want to thank Rodney King for his courage and fortitude. Over the years I have also been aided by the dedication and fine work of many lawyers and law clerks, among them Miles Washington, Arthur Mitchell, Elizabeth Heller-Eto, Gayla Libet, Heidi Rand, Nedra Shawler, Michael Johnson, Patricia Ector, David Briggs, and Brenda Harbin Forte—who is now a judge.

My work and knowledge have constantly been enhanced by the efforts of my special police practice consultants, Deputy Chief Earl Sanders and Donald P. Van Blaricom; and my longtime private investigators, Harvey Yarborough and Charles Levenberg.

Many dedicated and insightful men and women in the media have furthered the cause. I am thankful to Lorraine Howell, Ross McGowan and KTVU, and Aleta Carpenter of KDIA—the "Boss of the Bay," with whom I did "Legally Speaking." Fred Beauford has done important work with me as a journalist, helping to bring police misconduct issues to light. Special thanks to Geraldo Rivera, not just for me, but on behalf of the many African-American lawyers who have found an open forum on his program.

My loyal and supportive staff make every day possible. Arlene Branch, Theresa Anderson, Dee Martini, Patricia Beane, Arlene Gonzalez, Joseph Zingale, Pamela King, Ann Rabun, Cheri King, Jacquie Wilson, Gail Bishop, and Michele Redding are fundamental to the work.

I am grateful to all of those people who made this book possible: my literary agent, Sherry Arden, who first believed in its importance, and Barbara Bacnel, who introduced me to Sherry; my co-author, Catherine Whitney, who enabled me to make my thoughts resonate on the page; Catherine's partner, Paul Krafin, who contributed his writing and research talents to the project; Catherine's agent, Jane Dystel, who lent her skill to the process; and my editor, George Witte, who placed his faith in me when others were skeptical.

Many others lent their time and talents to this book. Paul Whitney's photographs and interviews helped to bring the stories and the subjects to life. Lynn Lauber added her skill to the text, and Al Fariello spent many long hours transcribing tapes. I am also immensely appreciative of the contributions made by many fine citizens, including Robert Davis, Darrell Hampton, Doug Stevens, Brenda Curry, Otis Stillwell, Willard Stillwell, Hattie Stillwell, Betty Thomas, Charles Yoakum, LaDona Sumler, Mary Trahan, Joyce Sept, Patrick Simon, Anthony Knuckles, Kedar Ellis, Diallobe Johnson, Barbara Dean, and Officer Derrick Norfleet.

Foreword

A HOPE
OF HEALING

It takes a lot to make a grown man cry. I'm not talking about crocodile tears, or the emotions that spill over in times of joy and sorrow. I'm talking about the kind of tears that are churned up in the face of brutality and ignorance; tears that originate someplace deep in a man's gut after he has been beaten down and humiliated in front of his children. It's a hard thing to watch. When you see it, you want to turn your head away in embarrassment.

As a civil-rights attorney, the abuse of dignity is my daily fare, so I've witnessed that crying more times than I can count. With blacks, Hispanics, Asians, even whites. No single race can lay sole claim to the experience of humiliation. But mostly I've seen it with blacks. We don't like to hear it, and we don't want to believe it, but there's still an element in our society that feels a need to bring the black man down. When that element wears the shield of the law, the consequences can reverberate across generations, leaving permanent scars.

Blue vs. Black is the story of the conflict that goes on every day in the cities of America, between police officers and black citizens. The realities of the conflict can be ugly, the circumstances painful. But it is not my goal merely to display a catalog of horrors and leave them to simmer. I intend this book to be a platform for a national conversation about solutions. For while some may view this problem as impossible to solve, I am not among them. There is a solution to every human conflict. It only requires the will to pursue it.

During the past twenty years, I have represented hundreds of people in lawsuits involving allegations of police misconduct. You will meet some of them here, and will be impressed by their remarkable spirit. What is most notable about my clients is that they are not, for the most part, the type of people who would ever have reason to be involved in police actions. Most of them are solid citizens, ordinary people going about their business, just like you and me. They include a psychologist, a janitor, a social worker, the director of a community center, a grandmother, a retired Marine, several college students, a high-school coach, a secretary, a small-business owner, and even a police officer. The circumstances that landed them in the center of their personal nightmares were generally innocuous—a traffic stop, a jaywalking ticket, a stroll through the "wrong" neighborhood, a case of mistaken identity that could have been resolved in an instant. Sometimes it was nothing more than just being there: "walking while black," we call it; or "DWB"—driving while black. My clients over the years have confirmed the truth in the old cliché: Bad things *do* happen to good people.

However, it isn't a simple matter of black and white, righteousness versus abuse. The police officers involved in these confrontations cannot be painted in the broad strokes of a stereotype. It would be easy, of course, to peg them as rotten apples, bad cops, racists—dissolving their individuality behind the color blue, just as my clients' individuality has been dissolved behind the color black.

Although there is a minority of brutal cops in every precinct (estimated at 3 to 5 percent), the heart of the conflict is more complex than the misbehavior of a few. The challenge to define the source of the problem beneath the multilayered realities is the work of my life—and the task of this book.

The search for solutions goes to the heart of the police culture, where policy is set, attitudes are formed, and accountability is measured.

Imagine the result if enough people were committed to work for the day when blacks and cops might become allies, not enemies. When leaders on both sides preached cooperation rather than conflict. When citizens were shown respect by police officers, and returned it in kind. When public officials were held accountable for their mandate to protect and serve. When a basic sense of trust and common purpose existed between cops and communities.

These are possible goals. But they require an ability to see all sides of every issue—to be clearheaded when our hearts feel outrage. They require a will for change, a blueprint. In Chapter 14 of this book, I will present my own 10-point proposal that I have shaped in consultation with leading experts on police policy and procedures.

While I was writing this book, I recontacted many of the people whose stories are represented in the following pages. To be perfectly honest, I didn't know what I would find. In some cases, many years had passed since we had spoken. I expected resistance—a reluctance to revisit what were very painful episodes. I also expected a certain reticence about identification. I was prepared to mask their identities, to save them further anguish. They were, however, eager to talk, to stand up and be counted, to let their names and faces provoke dialogue and produce change. These men and women were able to pull from the depths of their bruised psyches the courage to be a part of the solution. It's a start.

—John Burris
September 1999

Chapter 1

A MAN WHO CRIED

We have ground the manhood out of them,
and the shame is ours not theirs.

—MARK TWAIN

Robert Davis was a man in his forties who worked as a janitor in the Oakland school district. One afternoon, Davis drove to the Wells Fargo Bank to take care of some business, and he brought along his three-year-old daughter. She loved going in the car with Daddy, as all kids

Robert Davis's smile could light up a room. He was an ordinary man, and he was black.

do. After they finished at the bank, she was being a little rambunctious. She tried to jump into the car before Davis could lift her, and she slipped and fell onto the sidewalk. She wasn't really hurt, but she was crying a little, and when Davis picked her up, he noticed a bump on her head. He decided to drive to the hospital to make sure she was okay. As he strapped her into the car seat, a couple of women who were watching from nearby got it into their heads that maybe this man was kidnapping the little girl since she was crying. They called the police.

So Davis was driving along and all of a sudden there was a police car racing up behind him, with sirens blaring and lights flashing. Davis instinctively moved toward the side to let them pass. It didn't enter his mind that the car was chasing *him*. He wasn't speeding or anything. But the police car stayed behind him, and after a couple of blocks he finally figured out that they must be following him, so he pulled over and stopped. Two cops jumped out of the car and rushed up to Davis's driver's-side door.

"What's the problem, officers?" Davis barely got the words out of his mouth before the cops had pulled his door open. They yanked him from the car, and without another word one of the cops blasted him with a stun gun. He hit the ground, then in a pained daze tried to get up. His daughter was screaming with terror, and Davis, stumbling and disoriented, tried to reassure her. "I'm all right, baby. Daddy's all right." He felt an overwhelming need to go to her and protect her.

Davis was almost on his feet when the cop sent another

wave of electricity blazing from the stun gun.* As electricity surged through Robert Davis, he sank to the ground. The prongs were locked on, and he could no longer find his feet.

One of the officers approached him, roughly pulled his arms behind him, and cuffed him. Then he was dragged to the back of the police car and shoved inside. Davis had been subjected to thousands of volts of electricity. He was burned and in shock; he couldn't even speak. Neither of the police officers had told him yet why he had been pulled over. Neither of the officers had asked him for any information or identification. His daughter was screaming for her daddy. And not a word had been said to Robert Davis about why this was happening.

A few weeks after this incident, Davis and his wife came to my office. They walked in, holding hands, and seemed to be very loving and devoted to each other. Davis was an ordinary blue collar kind of guy, about five foot ten, maybe two hundred pounds, with a slight paunch and glasses. He flashed an engaging smile, so sweet and genuine that it lit up the room. There was nothing about him that appeared threatening or surly. He looked down at his lap while he was telling me his story, and I could see that tears were starting to glisten under his eyelids. He was so ashamed that his innocent daughter had had to witness this incident—that he couldn't protect her. It never fails. The *victim* is always ashamed.

---

*A brief note on stun guns, commonly referred to as Tasers. One application of 50,000 volts will disable the most deranged, most determined attacker. There is also an aural display that accompanies the application—the sound of crackling electricity. The prongs that shoot out and attach to the target to deliver the Taser's charge, also burn the flesh. If left attached, as they were in Robert Davis's case, the prongs cause severe burns.

My initial instinct, my gut response, was anger. I was so outraged that I wanted to get even for what had happened to this man. But instead, I took a deep breath and applied my training and experience. I forced my head to quiet the pleadings of my heart. I set aside my emotional reaction and reserved my judgment. I had learned never to take a story at face value. I wasn't there; I didn't see what happened. When people get excited, they sometimes blow things out of proportion. Or they fail to mention that they had been drinking, or in possession of drugs, or had physically resisted the police. A cop has the right to respond to these circumstances.

So the first thing I did after Davis and his wife left, was to call together my "rollout team." My team was made up of a couple of retired veteran cops who worked as private investigators, and a photographer who specialized in capturing the crucial details of a scene. Together we set out to discover as much as we could about Robert Davis and what really had happened to him.

Perhaps the most important thing we wanted to find out was this: What was the perspective of the police officers involved? Did Robert Davis do anything that might have led them to behave as they did? Even if the officers had made a mistake, did they make a wrong choice for the right reason? Were the officers following standard procedures? Were their actions reasonable under the circumstances?

That's why I use former cops as investigators. They've experienced similar situations and know what can happen in the heat of the moment. They intuitively understand what a cop's reasonable response might be. In the Davis incident, my investigators assured me that the cops didn't seem to have behaved reasonably, based on the given set of circumstances. Davis had pulled over and stopped his car. He wasn't acting hostile, just curious. Why hadn't the police officers questioned him? They might have said, "We had a report that a little girl was hurt." They could have spoken to the child and asked her, "Is this your daddy? Are you okay?" Instead, acting on the report of a *possible* kidnapping by a couple of highly agitated bystanders, the officers had made some very rash judgments. They had drawn a conclusion and reacted before they had any actual evidence of wrongdoing.

As we continued to investigate, we learned that Robert Davis was a solid citizen. He'd never been in trouble with the law. In fact, he seemed to be a real prince of a man. He loved his wife, adored his two daughters, and was devoted to his mother. He was a deacon at his church—the same little family church of twenty-five people he'd been going to since he was a boy. The teachers at the schools where he was a janitor couldn't say enough good things about him—how the kids all loved him, how he'd do anything for you, how he took so much pride in making the buildings shine. Everyone we talked to was shocked that this could have happened to Robert Davis.

So I eagerly took on Robert Davis's case. He was by all accounts a *good* guy, who had been pulled out of his normal, everyday life, and assaulted. He had been confronted by two police officers, rendered senseless without a word from them, and painfully robbed of his dignity. He had been treated like a dangerous criminal in front of his child. Passersby who saw the incident no doubt thought, *That black guy must be really violent. Why else would two cops shoot him continuously with 50,000 volts of electricity?*

When Robert Davis was finally given his day in court, my job was to introduce him to the mostly white jury as a good man—just like them. I wanted the jurors to see *the person* this terrible thing had happened to. To help them get past the stereotypes about race and class. To let them know how he had been hurt, not just physically, but in a more penetrating way—psychologically. In order to give the jurors a sense of what a decent man Davis was, I brought in all the teachers from the schools he worked at, the preacher from his church, the folks in his neighborhood, and I let them tell the jury about Robert Davis.

During the trial I also played a tape-recording of the sound a stun gun makes when it's activated. It's a sickening sound— somewhere between the violent crack of a bullwhip and the spitting, snarling hiss and sizzle of a high-voltage wire dancing on the ground after it's been downed in a storm. The jurors flinched with each crack. I ran the tape for the same amount of time that Robert Davis had been jolted by the stun gun. Davis sat at the plaintiff's table, clenching his hands and grimacing with real pain as the sound of his torment was replayed. I told the jury that being continuously zapped by a stun gun felt like being electrocuted.

When Davis took the stand and started to talk about what had happened, his voice cracked. He was a proud man, and he was ashamed of his tears, but they came anyway, sliding down his cheeks. He looked into my eyes and his voice was full of hurt. "Why did they *do* me that way, Mr. Burris? Why couldn't they just talk to me? I'm not a criminal. I'm not violent. Why did they *do* me that way?"

I knew the answer. Because they *could*.

The jury awarded Davis $25,000. It wasn't much in the scheme of things. What price do you place on an experience like that? How many people want to be nearly electrocuted? Who would do that for the money? In a civil trial, money becomes the currency of justice. The court equates the awarding of money with that justice, and the payment is retribution for the respect that was withheld in the first place. Robert Davis wasn't looking for any of this to happen. Respect was all he ever wanted.

This turned out to be an extraordinary case in one regard. After the verdict was reached, one of the police officers who had been in the car that day, approached Davis and took his hand. "I want to say how sorry I am," the officer said. "This shouldn't have happened. I hope things go all right for you." I think that officer's apology meant a lot more to Davis than the money did. It's the only time I've ever heard a cop say he was sorry.

DAVIS IS EVERYMAN

Robert Davis was an ordinary man—no more, no less— and when this incident occurred, there was nothing he could do about it. You might think, *At least he got justice in court. The system worked.*

But did it?

Robert Davis won in court, but that wasn't true justice.

True justice occurs when a person can come to court and have his case heard in a setting free of preconceived notions about race or class. True justice happens in an environment where police officers are not automatically presumed to be telling the truth—when a citizen's complaint can be weighed in equal balance. We haven't arrived at that point yet. Had Robert Davis's character been an iota less sterling, his chances of receiving a fair hearing would have been dramatically lessened.

From my point of view, Robert Davis's experience is not one man's travel on an isolated road that leads to nowhere. This is a road that is similar to what a lot of lawyers in a lot of different urban centers are grappling with. Robert Davis represents many different cases. He is the invisible man in our culture.

If someone like this could be treated so egregiously, what hope could there be for a black person who was engaged in criminal activity? Our constitution provides due process for every citizen, even a criminal. Yet most people are relatively indifferent to reports of police officers administering street justice, even though their actions challenge the very foundation of our democracy.

It was an honor to represent Robert Davis. He is good and decent—with a special quality about him I'll never forget. He epitomizes what has happened to black men for as long as I can remember, back to the days when I was a kid watching the civil-rights movement unfold in front of my eyes in Little Rock, Arkansas, and Selma, Alabama. I was young then, and I was safe in my stable home, in my working-class town of Vallejo, California. But I saw the scenes on TV—the firehoses,

12

the dogs, the beatings, and the lines of brave people, locking arms and singing even as they were roughed up and cut down. The old spirituals rose from their midst, the deep contralto tones mingling with the shouts and cries: *"We shall overcome someday."*

It left an impression on me, that the police could abuse their authority and hurt good and ordinary people. That they could use the badge as a shield against their own misdeeds. I had not experienced it myself, but I knew it to be true.

Something moved very deep inside of me as I watched Robert Davis, crying on the stand and asking me in a choked voice, "Mr. Burris, why did they do this to me?" And as he wept, the all-white jury stared at him, dispassionate. His wife and daughter looked on with tightened mouths, tears slowly rolling down their faces.

A grown man crying. I will always remember two things about Robert Davis—the light of his smile and the pain of his tears.

It broke my heart, and deepened my resolve.

Chapter 2

BLACKS AND COPS IN CONFLICT

Power never takes a back step—only in the face of more power.

—Malcolm X,
Malcolm X Speaks

The conflict between cops and blacks has hardened to the point where solutions seems as ephemeral as dust in the wind. The current standoff is the legacy of too many failures; promises from on high that don't make it to the street; political agendas on both sides; and lies told from a place of ideology, personal gain, indifference, and ignorance. It is distrust passed on from generation to generation like an evil talisman. Sadly, the few voices on each side of the conflict who are most resistant to solutions, drown out the rest, and in this way they make the gully seem too deep to cross. Others stand back in silence, usually out of fear, or out of a cold reckoning with the reality that has been their experience.

Recently a young black man, still smarting from the psychic wounds inflicted years earlier by a police officer who was too swift with a baton and too slow to reason, remarked, "I tell the kids, stay down. Don't be fuel for the fire. [The police are] out there like a taunting presence, and they want to pull you into a confrontation." His words chilled me, because they weren't spoken cynically. He was just being practical.

In the midst of the Los Angeles riots that followed the acquittal of police officers involved in the Rodney King beating, a police officer expressed an attitude that has become a mantra of police officers in their contact with citizens: "How can you expect us to respect these people when they don't even respect themselves?" *"These people"*! Who the hell was he talking about? Me? My sister? Robert Davis? All of us? I realized that a black face would always represent "these people" to him.

Cops and blacks each spin their mythologies on separate but parallel tracks. Police abuse solidifies anger, hopelessness, and fear. Sometimes it leads to violence. Cops, in turn, justify their actions by holding high the lawlessness of a few as an excuse to suspend the rights of the innocent. Entrenched as warriors in opposing foxholes, the two sides wait for their moments.

And so it goes, as our nation practices a selective blindness. In this great and strong nation, we have all become unwitting accomplices to the continuation of the conflict.

For too long, we have allowed ourselves to believe that our country has grown out of its former biases—that the past years of racial hatred have at last been stored away in our shameful past. We have been comforted in the belief that it's unthinkable in this day and age that a black man could be tortured by a state-sanctioned mob. We were sickened by the videotape of police officers beating Rodney King, but we convinced ourselves it was an isolated incident. If this sort of thing happened all the time, we'd *know* about it, wouldn't we?

The truth is, we *do* know about it. But in this great land where life, liberty, and the pursuit of happiness are the highest values, we do not treat every citizen equally. We view blacks as a seamless mass, not as individuals. We tar all blacks with the lawless acts of the few.

ACROSS THE LAND

The problem is national, and to a large extent it is rooted in the atmosphere, attitudes, policies, and practices of police departments. In urban areas, especially, there is a sentiment that the community is a law-enforcement landmine. The result is that many officers who could become role models for the young, unformed minds in those communities, instead become objects of fear and resentment. Once people have experienced brutality from any one cop, there is a tendency to assume that every cop is brutal. This may not be reasonable, but it is an understandable, visceral reaction.

After the L.A. riots in the aftermath of the Rodney King criminal verdict, the Christopher Commission (named for former Secretary of State Warren Christopher) was formed to evaluate the LAPD. The commission's report was highly critical of what it called "rampant police misconduct," with very few internal controls. On the training of officers, LAPD commander Michael Bostic, assigned by Chief Daryl Gates to review all LAPD training following the Rodney King incident, was quoted as saying, "I don't think there is any FTO training in this organization. Field training officers are made field training officers on a Friday afternoon, and Monday they go to work."

As to punishing problem officers, Commander Bostic told the commission, "I've interviewed several hundred people in the organization, from lieutenants and captains and all of the commanders and deputy chiefs, and [there's a] kind of a recurring theme that I've heard that's really bothered me. . . . They say that the organization is light on excessive force. . . . Light in punishment. And, I then said to them, 'Well, what do you mean?' and almost universally they gave me these examples. They said, 'If you lie, cheat, and steal, we'll fire you; if you use drugs, we'll fire you. But if you use excessive force, we won't.' "

Several years ago, the Mollen Commission, which was formed to study police corruption in New York City, found that excessive force and assault were commonplace in the police force. As one officer, nicknamed "The Mechanic" for his skill in beating people up, testified, "We'd just beat people in general. . . . To show who was in charge." The Mollen Commission also found that lying under oath was so rampant among police officers, they had coined a word for it—"testilying."

In Philadelphia a task force appointed by the police commissioner ten years ago to study police misconduct made recommendations that remain unenforced to this day. In large part, according to many observers, this is due to the strong resistance of the police union and its supporters in city and state government. Police unions can wield tremendous power when it comes to having charges dismissed, forcing the reinstatement of officers who have been fired, and overturning the findings of Internal Affairs divisions.

In Boston, the St. Clair Commission, appointed by the mayor to study allegations of police brutality, submitted a report in 1992 detailing substantial problems in the leadership and management of the police department. Community confidence was so low, the commission called for the resignation of then–police commissioner, Francis Roache. Of particular concern were the "shoddy, halfhearted investigations" conducted by the Internal Affairs Division. According to the commission report, "Given the Internal Affairs Division's failure to routinely provide thorough and timely investigations of alleged misconduct, and the fact that the department sustains less than 6 percent of complaints against officers, it is no surprise that the overwhelming majority of community residents we spoke to have little confidence in the department's ability or willingness to police itself."

In the aftermath of such reports, along with national appeals for an end to police brutality, many cities have instituted improvements. However, it is questionable whether or not these improvements penetrate the bedrock police culture.

In June 1998, the organization Human Rights Watch, a division of Amnesty International, released a detailed report on police brutality in fourteen U.S. cities: Atlanta, Boston,

Chicago, Detroit, Indianapolis, Los Angeles, Minneapolis, New Orleans, New York, Philadelphia, Portland (Oregon), Providence, San Francisco, and Washington, D.C. The report cited excessive use of force, primarily directed against blacks and Hispanics. "Police officers engage in unjustified shootings, severe beatings, fatal chokings, and unnecessarily rough physical treatment in cities across the United States," it said. "Their police superiors, city officials, and the Justice Department fail to act decisively to restrain or penalize such acts, or even record the magnitude of the problem."

The report further stated that Attorney General Janet Reno's Justice Department has thus far failed to comply with a 1994 requirement that the Justice Department collect data on police use of excessive force. Human Rights Watch Executive Director Kenneth Roth called the Department's data-collection efforts "carefully calculated to avoid tackling the problem head-on. They are thinly disguised exercises in irrelevancy."

Discouraging reports like these rekindled in my mind my early days as a lawyer in Chicago, when I was a volunteer with the Metcalfe Commission. It was the first full-fledged study of police misconduct, and it served as a real eye-opener for me. At that time, filled with the righteous certainty that only the young possess, I believed the Metcalfe Report would so inflame the citizenry, that police misconduct against blacks would be forever abolished. I was wrong. But it astounds me that in the 1990s, these reports are becoming so commonplace that they barely warrant a front-page headline.

It's no wonder that there is such a state of tension and

conflict between black communities and cops. Think about it and you begin to see all the signs of a relationship that has failed. Now it's become a vicious cycle. When a police officer behaves in a disrespectful, arbitrary, and possibly violent way toward a citizen, that citizen (along with his family, his friends, and anyone who observed the incident) is going to feel he can't trust the police. The next time he has an encounter with a cop, he's probably going to be suspicious, reluctant to cooperate, and even disrespectful. This attitude will only frustrate and anger the cop, and perhaps lead to an incident that will drive the two sides even farther apart. And on it goes, until an entire community and police force are caught up in this hostile tango.

No one wants to believe police misconduct is possible. Because if you start believing the police are capable of hurting you, your entire sense of security is shattered. Who do you call when you're injured or scared? Who do you call when the bad guys are knocking at your door? Many black people I know are afraid to call the police when they're in danger. It's like Little Red Riding Hood running away from the wolf to Grandma's house, only to find that Grandma *is* the wolf.

THE COST OF ABUSE

We are accustomed to measuring the cost of police brutality in terms of the physical wounds and psychological scars suffered by the victims. And there is always a level of disagreement between the two sides about that. What I cannot understand, however, is why level heads within police departments are not more alarmed by the dollars-and-cents cost of police brutality.

The recent Human Rights Watch report, for example, catalogued the cost (in settlements and other awards) of police brutality and misconduct in several major cities.

- The New York City Police Department paid about $70 million between 1994 and 1996 to settle complaints from citizens against police officers for assault/excessive force, assault/false arrest, shootings by police, and false arrest. In approximately 90 percent of those cases, the lawsuit was not recorded in the officer's personnel file because the city's Law Department and Internal Affairs determined the officer was acting within the scope of his or her duty. In other words, approximately $63 million was paid out without any consequences to those involved.

- The Los Angeles Police Department paid $34.3 million in settlements and lawsuit awards between 1994 and 1996. Prior to 1998, Internal Affairs prescreened all civil lawsuits, and only investigated those that were found by the department to involve misconduct. Today, all claims against officers initiate internal investigations. The effectiveness of this is still in question, considering that of 561 civilian complaints forwarded to the department in 1995, not a single one was sustained.

- In Washington, D.C., there is no formal notification procedure whereby the city's corporation counsel notifies the police department about civil suits being filed against officers. The approximately $4 million spent on settlements, primarily out-of-court, between 1993 and 1995 (the latest figures available), was treated by the city as the cost of doing business—and rarely translated into disciplinary actions against officers.

· Between 1992 and 1997, the city of Chicago reportedly paid more than $29 million to settle 1,657 lawsuits involving excessive force, false arrest, and improper search allegations; this figure does not include damages awarded in civil trials— a number that has not been made available. Again, the cost of settling lawsuits has had little effect on the police officers involved, since their supervisors often are not informed of the complaints.

· Between July 1, 1995, and April 1, 1997, the city of Detroit paid nearly $20 million in cases involving excessive force, wrongful deaths, and other misconduct—and the annual average over the past ten years has remained steady at about $10 million. Lawsuits are paid out of the city's fund, and Internal Affairs does not launch its own investigation after a lawsuit is filed.

· Even San Francisco, a small and relatively progressive city, regularly pays upward of $1 million to settle citizen lawsuits against police officers. And Oakland, which is half the size of San Francisco, averages nearly $2 million a year.

These are alarming numbers. But what is truly baffling is that there is virtually no correlation made between the money spent and the individuals who precipitate these actions. If you consider this scenario occurring in a large company, imagine how different the response would be. Say twenty or even just one or two individuals within your company regularly cost you a quarter million dollars, a half million dollars, or one hundred thousand dollars. Can you imagine saying, "We paid the money, but he [or she] wasn't really at fault"? Worse, can you imagine saying, "We're not going to find out why he or she is costing us so much money"?

Or would you say, "This guy is costing us too much"?

I suspect that if these numbers were highlighted regularly in the press, taxpayers would demand accountability—but the high cost of police misconduct is rarely made public. Settlements are normally handled quietly and receive little, if any, press attention. In spite of the catalog of abuses, the mainstream press tends to be overly accommodating toward police departments. Perhaps this merely reflects the mood of the population at large—as evidenced by the popularity of shows like *Cops*. For example, the city of Indianapolis rarely settles civil claims against police officers out of court; there is such a high level of pro-police sympathy on the part of jurors, that few cases are successful.

Consider this. The dust had barely settled in the Rodney King case when Carlos Moorhead, a Republican congressman from California, introduced a bill in the House of Representatives, titled, The Law Enforcement Officers' Civil Liberty Act. The intent of the bill was to make it harder for citizens to sue police officers. The bill called for a reduction in the amount of attorney fees that could be paid to represent a citizen in a misconduct suit against a police officer (thus discouraging lawyers from taking civil-rights cases), as well as creating a legal limit of $10,000 in punitive-damage awards. Furthermore, the bill would have drastically increased evidentiary requirements by asking if an officer had "intended" to cause serious injury.

As a "solution" to the growing cost of police brutality, this legislation was painfully misguided. Congressman John Conyers, Jr., a Democrat from Michigan who led the opposition, stated, "This bill should be called, 'The Rogue Cop Bill of Rights.' It's a slap in the face of every victim of police abuse. It's the worst possible way to deal with growing police misconduct."

Moorhead's bill never gained momentum, but it is indicative of a segment within government and law enforcement that believes challenging police misconduct and abuse is a form of disloyalty to the men and women who serve our communities. As long as the sentiment exists that police officers are above the law that they are charged with enforcing, there will be a price. In the short term, that cost will be paid out of city coffers. In the long term, the cost will be reflected in the eyes of children who grow up fearing and mistrusting law-enforcement personnel.

It is easy to forget, in the land of the numbers-crunchers and statistical analysts, that each complaint wears a human face; each dollar paid represents a price much higher than money.

Chapter 3

THE MEASURE OF A MAN

The measure of a man is not how he stands during times of comfort and convenience, but how he stands in times of strife and discord.

—Dr. Martin Luther King, Jr.

When I was growing up in Vallejo, California, it felt like everyone in our little town was a relative or a friend. Like my parents, many blacks had moved there from the South to work at the Mare Island Naval Base. When I was born in 1945, Vallejo was already 30-percent black. It was a close-knit community with very little crime. It was your typical black neighborhood then. Mothers and fathers in the home. Stable government jobs. Although racism was openly sanctioned in those days, I never really felt its sting. We were poor, but not dirt-poor, and I never thought we were inferior. In fact, my grandmother and my mother seemed like the most powerful two people in the world.

We worked, we played, and for extra money, we picked fruit. I was so innocent. For me it was an adventure—all of us piling into my dad's rickety old truck, riding north to the lush, heavily scented fields. We picked peaches, pears, and prunes in the summer; grapes and apples in the fall; walnuts in November. My dad had a regular job at the naval base, but with six kids to feed and my mother's propensity to take in anyone who needed help, the extra money came in handy. Maybe it was a natural consequence of living surrounded by orchards and vineyards and fields bursting with nature's bounty. Maybe it was because my family once worked in the cotton fields of Oklahoma. But sometimes I wonder if all those hot summer days, long weekends, and late autumn nights in the fields weren't my parents' way of teaching us kids a vital lesson. Toiling alongside the migrant workers, who set up temporary residence in makeshift shacks on the edge of the fields, we had a glimpse of what we didn't want to be. The experience planted something that would forever linger in our memories—the long shadows cast by the white field-bosses standing over us.

The message wasn't clear to me then. I was happily innocent. But by the time I got to junior high school, I began to notice a few lopsided realities. All of us, black and white, were so close as kids. But as we grew older we became separated by unspoken social custom. I felt that I was different—treated one way on the sports field, and another way socially. My white teammates continued their bond off the field, but I wasn't included in that side. It wasn't because the kids were mean or hated blacks. That was just a time when the races were separated. The older I got, the more apparent it became, and the more it bothered me.

I also began to notice that there were two career tracks at my high school—one for blacks and one for whites. My teachers encouraged my passion for sports, and pushed me toward classes like shop and mechanics. Meanwhile I noticed that most of my white friends were being directed toward the college-preparatory courses, the classes that would lead to professional careers. When a teacher I liked casually mentioned that I probably wouldn't be going to college, I took it as a challenge. I decided to show him how wrong he was.

And so I became the first person in my family to go to college, and that should have kept me busy enough. But it was soon clear that I didn't know what the hell I was doing. I got married and had a kid when I was nineteen. That's what everyone I knew did. But how could I handle a marriage when I was trying to deal with college at the same time? Besides, I had no direction in my life. The marriage lasted less than a year. Meanwhile everyone in my family was telling me to choose a nice, safe profession. Well, I listened to that advice, and I took it. That's how I ended up being an accountant. I got hired as the first black in a fancy accounting firm in downtown San Francisco, and my boss used to tell me, "You're the Jackie Robinson of accounting"—an image that grated on me more than I can say.

Apart from my facility with numbers, I couldn't have chosen a career for which I was more poorly suited. Everything about working for an accounting firm rubbed me the wrong way, went against the grain of my interests and personality. It bored me to death. There I was in the late 1960s, living on the edge of Berkeley, California—ground zero for the revolution that was at hand, and the home of the Black Panthers—and I was working in a profession whose primary aim was to be as bland as the woodwork.

When I left the world of accounting and headed for law school in Berkeley, I felt tremendously relieved, as if I had miraculously escaped a fate worse than death. Now I could deal with what was going on all around me. I grew the obligatory afro and got involved in a few student organizations, where I assumed leadership positions. I was always listening, soaking in information. When I heard the thundering rhetoric of Bobby Seale, Stokely Carmichael, and Huey Newton, I kept asking, "What does this mean for me? How can I apply it?" There was an analytical cast to my passion. I felt deeply that the law was the key. The way I saw it, the proper application of the law was the way to deal with the oppressive forces keeping the people down. Without the legal system there would be chaos. After law school, I decided to head for Chicago (a *real* city, in my opinion). It was quite a change of environment from the West Coast. I ultimately joined the Cook County state's attorney's office and suddenly found myself in the surreal position of being on the same side of the law as Mayor Richard Daley. I also had an experience that would percolate under the surface for many years, and finally form my choice of vocation. It was the time I spent volunteering for the Metcalfe Commission, the first full-fledged investigation into police misconduct, that educated me about the abuse of police official power.

Then, shortly after I finished with the commission, I observed the trial of the police officers who killed Fred Hampton, a Black Panther leader. The testimony rang true, showing that the police officers had ambushed, shot, and killed Hampton. It chilled me. As an assistant DA, I was on the side of law enforcement, but I had mixed emotions about whether I was on the side of justice.

I loved the energy of Chicago, but in 1977 I returned to Oakland. My son was twelve, and he needed me. I joined the Alameda County district attorney's office and tried to settle back into life in California. I was a low-burning engine, biding my time. My purpose was to be on the cutting edge of social issues, to be an advocate with a conscience. But I wasn't yet sure how it would happen—where in the scheme of change I belonged. I was passionate and outspoken, but I wasn't a firebrand. I loved to be heard, and I loved to argue the facts, but you wouldn't find me thundering revolution from a podium. Most of all, I read, watched, and listened as I developed an understanding of where *I* fit in. The truth is, I didn't want to be outside the system, pounding at the door. I thought I could do more from where I was. I still thought it was possible to straddle two worlds. I believed Martin Luther King's warning that "the measure of a man is how he stands in times of strife and discord." But my measure had not yet been taken.

MY CRUCIBLE

If a man is lucky, he can look back in time and point to a pivotal moment when his aspirations met his intentions—when his current life and future career came together for him. That moment seemed to be a long time coming for me. I was

almost thirty-four years old. My pivotal moment came because of Melvin Black, a fifteen-year-old boy unnecessarily
killed on a dead-end street in Oakland.

St. Patrick's Day, 1979

The city of Oakland was tense. Tempers had been at a hair
trigger for weeks. There had been a number of explosive confrontations between black citizens and cops. Several young
black men had been killed under questionable circumstances,
and there were numerous incidents of people getting roughed
up or beaten. It was a lose-lose situation: a bad time to be a
cop, a bad time to be a young black man. You got the feeling
that the next thing that happened would blow the city wide
open. But that wasn't on my mind as I drove over the Bay
Bridge on a March evening, coming home from a St. Patrick's
Day event in San Francisco. I was feeling good. At the end of
February, I'd left my job at the Alameda County district attorney's office, and I was now seventeen days into private
practice. I didn't have much in the way of a clientele, but at
least I was finally on my own. Like many former DAs, I was
switching tables and going into criminal defense, thinking my
passion for civil rights and justice could be fulfilled there.

As I slid past the tollbooths that fed highways in and out
of Oakland, a news flash came over the radio. "We have reports from motorists of a sniper shooting at cars on Highway
24 near the Grove Street on-ramp." My first thought was
relief. I'd already passed the area, so I was out of the sniper's
range. By the time I pulled into my driveway, the incident was
over, and a fifteen-year-old boy named Melvin Black was

dead—with eight bullet wounds in his back. The police had found their sniper.

But then the questions started pouring out of the community. Was Melvin Black really the sniper? He was standing outside of his own apartment building when he was confronted by police. The official statement was that Melvin had pointed a gun at police officers. But that didn't seem consistent with his being shot eight times in the back.

The community outrage finally provoked Oakland mayor Lionel Wilson to declare the appointment of an independent investigator into the death of Melvin Black. He offered the position to me, and I accepted. The truth is, I was elated. What a fantastic break! Two weeks into private practice and I was being handed a high-profile case. Besides, I knew I was the right guy for the job. As a former deputy DA, I was familiar with the police perspective. As a black man, I was sensitive to the mood of the community. And this was my meat. I loved the methodical, slow buildup of an investigation—putting the thousands of tiny pieces of an intricate puzzle together to form a conclusion. I knew Melvin Black was dead, but I didn't know *why* he was dead. I hadn't formed an opinion one way or another. But as the months went by, I would find out exactly what had happened that night.

I hired the renowned San Francisco investigator Hal Lipset, and we dissected the case piece by piece. We visited the scene so many times that it haunted my dreams. Let me say this about it: It was a sad place to die, a down-and-out dead-end street, set against a rocky hillside that led up to the freeway. Sunburned tufts of grass mixed with gravel, dilapidated buildings, and the steady roar of traffic from above.

We performed a nighttime reconstruction at the scene. It was very dark, with the barest flickering of light from the nearby buildings. I leaned against a car parked in front of Melvin's building—assuming the position that the officers had reported finding Melvin in that night. Dangling at my side, in my right hand, was a pellet gun.

A sudden flash of light cut into the dark street as a car drove slowly toward me. I was still in shadow when a voice ordered, "Police! Put your hands on the car," and another voice simultaneously shouted, "Police! Freeze!"

According to police reports, Melvin swung around and pointed his gun straight at them, then took off. They opened fire—*bang, bang, bang, bang, bang, bang, bang, bang*—eight shots. I ran, as Melvin had, away from the police, around the back of the buildings. Before I turned the corner, and while I was still running, I pointed the pellet gun back at the police. (It was virtually impossible to do this while running.) They followed—*bang, bang, bang*. I was down now, crawling toward a doorway, toward cover. *Bang, bang*.

I stood up and brushed off my sweatpants. I was panting as Hal joined me in the dark alleyway behind the building. "Those officers must have been shocked when they didn't find a gun on his body," he said quietly. I nodded, thinking hard. Melvin's pellet gun had later been discovered lying on the hood of the car. According to the police officers, they thought he still had it in his hand when he was running, but they suggested that he must have put it down after he pointed it at them the first time. The sequence didn't make sense.

The official version was that Melvin *a*) pointed his pellet gun at two fully armed police officers; then *b*) immediately turned to his left and placed the gun on the hood of the car; then c) turned back around to his right and started running away in a hunched position, at some point reaching his right hand back over his left shoulder, appearing to be pointing a gun back at them. But since the gun had actually been left on the hood of the car, Melvin could not have been trying to fire at them.

A sad place for a child to die.

According to the autopsy report, the first barrage of bullets hit Melvin twice in the front and twice in the buttocks, indicating that he had turned away to the right immediately. He would not have had time to place the gun on the car hood. He had most likely done it earlier—perhaps as soon as he saw the police car headed down the street. Furthermore, the officers had described a hunched-over, firing position. More likely, he was hunched over because he had already been hit.

Our investigation went on for five months, and we went over each detail again and again. It was an excruciating process. We had to be absolutely sure. The community wanted the truth, and we would not shortchange them by offering opinions. In the end, we were left with the troubling realization that the physical evidence did not match the officers' statements. The events simply could not have happened the way they had been reported.

It was not my place to judge the attitudes or motivations of the officers who killed Melvin Black. Maybe they were lying, maybe they had overreacted. I did know, however, that in the few moments it took for Melvin's life to end, these officers had repeatedly failed to follow departmental policy.

In September I filed a 700-page report. I really believed that the mayor and the city council wanted me to discover the truth about what happened to Melvin Black. That's what they had told the press; it's what the community expected. So when I turned in my report, I expected a full public disclosure.

Instead, there was silence. Several days passed. Then I got a call from someone at the mayor's office. He was seething. "The mayor has decided not to make the report public," he told me. "Christ, John, what the hell are you trying to do to us here?"

I wasn't a naive man. But perhaps I had mistaken the unspoken mandate of the investigation, and they hadn't expected such a harsh verdict from a former prosecutor who'd worked hand-in-hand with the cops all those years. Perhaps they'd figured that my being black would mollify the community when my report vindicated the police. But I didn't play that game; I didn't even know there *was* a game. So now all the powers-that-be—and all the cops—wanted my head.

That's when the scales dropped from my eyes. I saw the power of the law-enforcement bureaucracy, the ease with which facts could be manipulated, truth reinvented. I realized that if it could happen on this level, with the press and public watching every move, then surely it was impossible for an ordinary, anonymous citizen to get unbiased justice.

I was deeply disappointed by the lack of courage displayed by the public officials. Although portions of the report leaked out to the press, it wasn't until much later, when Melvin's family hired a lawyer and filed a civil suit, that the report saw the light of day as evidence in the suit. A jury awarded the family $693,000 for Melvin's wrongful death. It was a small vindication.

In the coming years, as I pursued my work in criminal law, Melvin Black was a light that burned steadily in the back of my consciousness. And it began burning brighter and brighter. I realized that civil-rights law would give me a chance to make an impact outside the four corners of a courtroom. Civil-rights law was about representing victims, not defendants. It was about redressing wrongs and holding people accountable. I began to change my focus to cases of discrimination and police misconduct.

For the first time in my life, I truly knew what my vocation was meant to be: to stand up for the citizens who were victimized—not necessarily criminals, but regular people going about their business; to be sure that official lies did not go unchallenged.

And I've been doing it ever since.

SOLUTIONS, NOT RHETORIC

I never believed, and I don't to this day, that *most* cops are bad. In fact, it's been my experience that there are only a handful in a department who are truly brutal. Other cops may be capable of an incident of abuse on a situational basis, but it's usually because they're scared, overexcited, or poorly trained.

The problem is, the few bad cops get away with it time and time again, in large measure because of the code of silence. I've talked to many police officers who felt sickened by what they had seen a brutal cop do, but the price for speaking out was simply too high. Clearly, the resolution of the problem begins with strong leadership in the law-enforcement hierarchy, and more careful attention to hiring, training, and evaluating police officers.

I reached that understanding long ago. For nearly twenty years, I have toiled away, patiently waiting for the cumulative impact of hundreds of incidents to finally ring out a clarion call to the nation. In October 1993, when I was asked by attorney Milton Grimes to join his team representing Rodney King in his civil trial against the city of Los Angeles, I thought there was an opportunity for the impact of this grave injustice to reach far beyond one man's life. I believed that a public enlightenment would occur—an understanding that the problem was deeper than a handful of brutal cops. But, although we won a large judgment for Rodney, the message was lost. By the time Rodney walked out of civil court, victorious, he was old news.

Besides, everyone seemed eager to blame the victim. People kept saying to me, "The police were wrong to beat up Rodney King, but he *was* breaking the law. He led them on a high-speed chase. He could have been on PCP." They wanted—no, they *needed*—to find an excuse for what happened because they couldn't believe that police officers would be so brutal if they didn't have *some* reason. Rodney King was by no means a saint. He wasn't on his way to church that night. But even a guy that you wouldn't want your sister to marry, has civil rights. He has human rights. He's not just a carcass on the pavement.

I was deeply frustrated and somewhat depressed when it was all over. I had expected a moment of national enlightenment, and it hadn't happened. And then the O. J. Simpson case exploded into the headlines, and suddenly the heat on black and white relations got turned up about a thousand degrees. I was listening to all the talk. I was also a big part of the talk—regularly appearing on *Rivera Live,* CNN, the morning programs, radio talk shows, and the like. The TV and radio hosts wanted to mix it up, get people yelling. I tried to be the voice of balance and reason in the midst of an unbridled emotional fever. The trouble was, no one wanted to be reasonable. It was all about choosing sides. Complete strangers were stopping me on the street to spontaneously argue their opinions about "the race card." A white man once accosted me in an airport and declared, "Because of the verdict, Colin Powell will never be president." It had never been my position that the LAPD framed O. J. Simpson. However, the LAPD was not blameless in the manner in which they conducted their investigation. What really disturbed me was the total lack of comprehension—on the part of white Americans—that such abuses by cops against black citizens can and do happen. I found it disheartening that the mostly black Simpson jury was scornfully dismissed as being biased and emotional. People cried, "Jury nullification!" When a mostly white civil jury found Simpson liable, the view of black versus white juries was solidified. Little note was given to the fact that the two juries were presented with different evidence and had a different burden of proof.

And I think Mark Fuhrman had a lot to do with the first verdict. I've often wondered if those good black citizens stared into Fuhrman's cold eyes and saw the look that haunted their own families, streets, and neighborhoods. It wasn't abstract for them. It was personal.

These abuses occur every day to law-abiding citizens. So you can begin to see why a black person might run when he sees a cop coming toward him; or why a driver might be nervous stopping along the highway when the police lights start flashing; or why someone would dare to speak back to a cop, maybe scream at him, "Why the hell did you do that?"

Police abuse is, to borrow a phrase from Ross Perot, "our crazy aunt in the attic." We all know she's there, but we keep her hidden. We need to bring her downstairs and deal with her, so that the vast majority of ordinary black citizens will not have to be the victims of her madness. We need to help her get better.

Chapter 4

WHAT CHILDREN SEE

You got people out there with this scar on their brains, and they will carry that scar to their graves. The mark of fear is not easily removed.
—ERNEST J. GAINES,
THE AUTOBIOGRAPHY OF MISS JANE PITTMAN

Most mornings, I'm out of the house by six. I unlock my sports utility vehicle and shove aside the kids' debris of sandwich wrappers, smashed paper cups, tennis rackets, and the like. I set my steaming coffee in the cup holder, slide in behind the wheel, and flick on the radio. Then I'm on my way, riding down from the Sequoia Highlands in the hazy morning sun.

I love the early part of the day before the huge octopus of intersecting freeways starts billowing its polluting forces of smoke and noise. Usually I avoid the freeways altogether and take Bancroft, a street which intersects the city, east to west. I turn on 98th Avenue and drive past Arroyo Park where the baseball teams I sponsored once played. In the stillness of the morning, the grass is dewy and fresh. The baseball diamonds gleam. Sadly, this park has been the scene of some of the worst police brutality cases I've handled. Ah, what children see.

It's a daily form of meditation for me, driving through the poor and lower-middle-class areas of East Oakland where the working folks live in row upon row of little one-story houses. These neighborhoods of Oakland always feel like home to me. When I was a kid, my mother and my grandmother used to drag us kids down from Vallejo every other Sunday for a daylong service at the Glorious Kingdom Primitive Baptist Church. This was serious soul-saving—hours of singing, praying, shouting, and preaching. I hated it with as much passion as others in the church reserved for Jesus. I wanted to be playing baseball and having fun, and it didn't seem fair to have to spend the *whole day* in church. Those dressed-up ladies with their big hats and clouds of perfume had a way of looking at me as if they'd just caught me in the act of disbelieving. They'd say, "Well, if it isn't John *L.*"—placing special emphasis on my middle initial. In that church, my name was John *L.*—like it was one word. It's funny. A lady from the church called me at my office a couple of years back. As soon as she said, "John *L.*," I started feeling guilty, remembering those days when I'd get caught sleeping in the back of the church. Even at fifty, hearing "John *L.*" made me sit up a little straighter in my seat.

The deepest sense of connection I feel with the people in these neighborhoods has to do with my work. I've represented so many of them in police-misconduct cases. Whenever anyone tries to feed me that tired old line about "violence in black communities," I tell them they've never been to Oakland. Like any other community, it's got pockets of problems. But for the most part, these are good, law-abiding, working people who keep their small plots of land impeccably neat and bursting with flowers. It raises my ire to hear these citizens spoken of with blind disrespect.

This particular morning, as I drive along, my thoughts are on a man named Darrell Hampton. I hadn't seen Darrell for a while, but I ran into him downtown the other day, and he's been on my mind ever since.

When I get downtown, instead of turning on Broadway toward my office, I make a right and drive into West Oakland. West Oakland has traditionally been the poorest and most troubled part of the city. Now there are early signs of gentrification. This is both good and bad news for the residents: good because the neighborhood is being cleaned up and improved; bad because its original residents won't have a prayer of enjoying the impressive changes. That's the problem with poverty. You have no purchase. As soon as your neighborhood starts getting fixed up, you get pushed out. You can't afford to live there anymore.

I turn on Adeline Street and slow down as I come to a block of ugly square buildings the color of pale mustard, that looks something like a prison encampment. It's the Acorn Housing Project. Not long ago, this was a bustling place, its 673 units fully occupied with low-income residents, but it's mostly empty now and scheduled to be torn down next year to make room for a high-rise. I make a left and drive into the project, along a narrow fire lane that runs straight through to

Darrell Hampton (outside the former Acorn Community Center, now being demolished): "I was 'Mr. Police.' "

the next block. There are concrete walkways extending from each building, leading to a large, open play area and a two-story building that was once the Acorn Community Center.

The fire lane cuts down the center of the play area. There are still a couple of remnants from the days when groups of children congregated here: a rusty jungle gym, an empty sandbox, a basketball hoop without a net.

I stop my car in front of the community center and sit there for a few minutes, sipping my coffee and thinking about Darrell. This was once Darrell's domain. That man was a *star*.

After five years as the director of the Acorn Community Center, Darrell Hampton had achieved folk-hero status. He was only five-ten, but he seemed to stand ten feet tall. He was handsome and strong—a runner and a weight lifter. He was one of those rare men who was like a force of nature; kids automatically trusted him and followed his path. When Darrell arrived on the scene in 1985, the housing project was known for being one of Oakland's prime trouble spots for drug use. But Darrell set out to change that, and it seemed he was achieving the impossible. Darrell's kids didn't do drugs.

They went on field trips—to museums, movies, baseball games. They participated in cultural exchange programs, such as trips to Mexico and even the Bahamas. They read books and watched movies. And they played sports. In 1990 Darrell was the proud guardian of an internationally ranked girls' track team.

The parents of these children could turn almost tearful when they spoke of Darrell. He was rescuing them from their worst nightmare. With Darrell in the picture they had hope again, that their beautiful babies would not grow hardened by the streets, feel the pull of the gangs, the allure of drugs. They could believe that their sons wouldn't be added to the statistics—dead or in prison by the time they were sixteen.

Darrell also taught the kids to believe that the police were their friends. Police, he would say, are the enemies of the bad guys, but they're here to help *you*. To further establish his point, Darrell frequently invited police officers in to give talks. He took groups to Police Athletic League activities and involved them in programs like "Take a Bite Out of Crime," and DARE.

On October 16, 1990, everything changed.

It was about three-thirty in the afternoon, and the playground was full of kids. Inside the recreation center, more kids were working the two pool tables and playing cards. Darrell was sitting on a sofa facing the Plexiglas window of the center, through which he had a full view of what was going on outside.

Suddenly Darrell heard the familiar sound of police sirens, and he saw a black-and-white zooming up the fire lane. Some of the kids inside the center started to run toward the door to see what was happening, and Darrell yelled for them to stay inside. He had never seen a police car move through the yard so fast, especially at this time of day when there were so many children around. He was shocked. A child could easily have been hit by the speeding car. He hurried out and stood on the top step, yelling for everyone to stay put.

At that moment, Elsie, a six-year-old who had been inside the center, came running out onto the steps and tugged desperately at Darrell's shirt. "Pooter's chasing me with the pool stick," she cried, pointing to an especially rambunctious five-year-old boy. Darrell turned back into the center and caught up with Pooter, who was waving the hind quarter of a collapsible pool cue—a thin little piece of wood about fourteen inches long. Darrell grabbed the pool cue out of Pooter's hand and returned to the front of the building. The police car had stopped a few yards away, but Darrell noticed that the reverse lights were on, as if the car was about to back up. Just then he saw a little girl, no older than four, running toward the fire lane. He yelled for her to stop. "Jump up on the toy, honey!" he called, motioning to the jungle gym. As she did, the police car came speeding backward down the lane, and stopped a few feet from the center steps.

"Hey," Darrell called to the cop in the car, "slow down. You have to take into consideration that little kids are playing here." The cop shrugged. He didn't seem to have any problem, and Darrell thought the incident was over. But just then, a chunky cop named Michael Yoell, came swaggering down the fire lane toward him. "And *you've* got to take into consideration that *you're* not a police officer," he said rudely.

Darrell looked at him quizzically. What was he talking about? "Being a police officer has nothing to do with speeding down the fire lane when there are kids playing," Darrell said. His reply seemed to spark a flame of rage in Yoell.

Michael Yoell was a big redhead, with a florid, unpleasant face and cold eyes, who had succeeded in making many people in the community afraid of him. He was known to treat blacks like dirt whether they were committing crimes or abiding by the law. Yoell had a record of twenty-six complaints from residents to the Oakland Police Department Internal Affairs Division for excessive use of force and racial misconduct. Charges included the time he stopped a black businesswoman who was making an illegal U-turn, dragged her out of her car, pulled her arm behind her back, and slammed her face into the hood of his police car. In another incident, he choked a man who had run a red light.

None of these complaints had been sustained by Internal Affairs. That means the department didn't find any of the complaints to be valid. Common sense alone would dictate that something was wrong here. Many cops *never* have misconduct or brutality complaints filed against them with Internal Affairs. Yet the department knew this guy was getting complaints all the time, and they thought nothing was amiss?

Darrell didn't know Officer Yoell, and if he had fully appreciated Yoell's tendencies, he might have mumbled some apologetic words and backed off. Then again, maybe he wouldn't have. There were at least thirty kids in the yard, and it was his responsibility to make sure none of them got hurt.

Yoell kept walking down the fire lane toward Darrell. "What's that in your hand?" he asked.

Surprised, Darrell looked down at his hand and realized he was still holding the collapsed pool cue. "Oh, this is just a pool cue from inside. I'm the community-center director."

"Drop it!" Yoell screamed.

"What?" Darrell didn't like the menacing way this cop was looking at him. He started backing up. "I told you, I work here."

"I don't care *where* you work," Yoell sneered, and then he lunged at Darrell and started choking him. The officer in the car, Alexander Boyovich—also notorious, with twenty-four complaints lodged against him with Internal Affairs—jumped out and ran over to assist. He pulled Darrell's arms behind his back and held him. Yoell stopped choking and started punching—five shots to the face, five shots to the ribs and stomach, then back to the face. By now, many of the kids had gathered around. They were shrieking and yelling, "Stop it! Stop hitting him!" Some of the smaller ones were sobbing in terror.

Two other officers, who had been chasing down a suspect in the projects, ran up to the scene. Now all four officers surrounded Darrell. He recognized one of them, a black officer named Johnson. All of the cops had stopped their previously crucial high-speed pursuit of an armed suspect, and decided instead to deal with Darrell's "attitude problem." The pool cue was their pry point, the excuse they used to leverage their irritation into violent assault.

Darrell felt a leg come up in front of him, and he tripped and fell down the two steps, hitting the asphalt face- and chest-first, and cutting his legs and knees. Yoell shouted, "Don't try to get up!"

Darrell didn't try to get up. He was barely conscious as he lay on the ground, blood pouring from his mouth. Then he felt a heavy foot or knee come down hard onto his lower back to hold him still while he was tightly handcuffed.

Darrell remembered very little once he was on the ground, but eyewitnesses said that he screamed out in agony as one cop came down on his back while another ground the heel of his boot into Darrell's neck. The witnesses also reported that Darrell was repeatedly kicked, punched, and struck with a heavy flashlight while apparently unconscious, and in secured police custody. The next thing Darrell *did* remember was being dragged to his feet by his armpits and yanked toward the back of a police cruiser, where other officers had gathered. As he looked up, he saw through bleary eyes a black police officer who was watching the scene from a short distance away— Victor Woods, an old classmate and friend. They'd played baseball together at El Cerrito High School. Their eyes met, but nothing was said.

The cops shoved him into the backseat of the car, next to a young man who was handcuffed. He turned out to be a kid from the projects, named Anthony, who had been arrested in a drug-related matter. Yoell uncuffed Anthony and let him go, then settled into the front passenger seat.

For the next few minutes, Yoell and Darrell were in the car alone.

"You out on parole or probation?" Yoell asked.

Darrell shook his head no. "I told you," he slurred through his swollen mouth, "I'm the director of the community center." Then, somehow Darrell had the presence of mind to tell Yoell that the keys to the center were in his pocket. "You have to give them to one of the adults so they can lock up."

Yoell reached back and pulled the keys and a wallet from Darrell's pocket. He pulled out the wallet's contents and threw everything on the dashboard, then started examining it, piece by piece. "You're some stupid idiot, you know that?" Yoell chuckled as he looked through Darrell's belongings. "Why'd you come after me like that with the pool stick?"

Darrell was stunned. What did Yoell mean? He never came after anybody. The cop was making it seem like Darrell had attacked him.

Yoell threw the rest of Darrell's papers on the dashboard and turned around in his seat. "Are you drunk, or does your breath always smell that bad?" he asked. Darrell didn't know how to respond to that, and he was in so much pain he could barely move or speak anyway. Yoell kept up his verbal jabbing. "You seem like you're a little inebriated."

"Inebriated"? How about beaten to a pulp? Darrell felt as if he was hearing the invention of a police report that would go something like, "Suspect was drunk. He lunged at police officer with a dangerous weapon."

Yoell was still staring at him, and his eyes were narrow with disdain. "You know why you're a stupid idiot? Because you don't get it. We can do anything to you we damn well want. If your attitude doesn't change, we'll come back out and beat you again."

Meanwhile, people had started surrounding the police car. There were forty or so kids and adults who had witnessed the beating, and they were furious, yelling, "There was no reason for that! You had no right to hurt that man. He didn't do anything wrong!" Boyovich jumped into the car and started the engine. "We're going to take this discussion to a back lot in the projects before there's a riot here." He drove around to a secluded lot where two other police cruisers were sitting, and several cops were milling around. Yoell and Boyovich got out and started talking to the others, and Darrell saw a Hispanic officer pointing to him and asking Yoell, "Don't you know who that is?"

For the next thirty minutes Darrell sat alone and handcuffed in the back of the police car while the officers discussed what to do about him. His initial shock had eased, and now he was really starting to feel the pain. His jaw was swollen and pounding, and his lip was still bleeding. His throat was very sore from Yoell's initial choking. He could also see blood coming through his pants legs, and his ribs felt so sensitive he thought they might be broken. The worst pain was in his lower back where the officer had knelt on top of him. He couldn't find a position to ease the intense throbbing because the handcuffs were holding his arms tightly behind him. It felt like the longest thirty minutes of his life.

Finally Yoell and Boyovich returned and started the car. Yoell asked Darrell if he wanted to be taken to Highland Hospital. He said no. He figured they were going to take him a few blocks away, out of sight of Acorn, and drop him off. Then he'd get someone to take him to Kaiser, a much better hospital where he had very good medical coverage. Besides, he didn't want to be taken to a neighborhood hospital. He was embarrassed enough without having to endure the added humiliation of being handcuffed to a hospital bed for several hours in full view of people who knew him.

So the police took Darrell to the Washington Street Police Station, and brought him into the jail. The guard looked at him snidely and asked, "Are you finished fighting?"

It hurt to talk, but Darrell managed to say, "I didn't fight *yet!*"

Without a word, the guard led him into a holding cell and left him there alone.

Darrell still didn't know that he was being arrested, since nobody had read him his Miranda rights yet. He struggled to make sense of what was happening, but a blinding headache and the pain of his wounds clouded his thoughts. He felt disconnected from reality. When an officer finally arrived to read him his rights and tell him he was being arrested, he thought it was a bad dream.

Meanwhile, on the street, there was furious activity from the local residents. As the word spread that Darrell had been beaten and taken away by the cops, people reacted with shock. The kids at Acorn were still hanging around the center, as if they hoped someone would tell them it had all been a joke. Maybe Darrell and the cops would arrive laughing and say, "Gotcha!" Denial can sometimes be the only protection a vulnerable child can cling to.

Within an hour after Darrell's departure, the phone lines were burning—to the mayor's office, the police department, and to local congressmen. The phone on my desk rang about six P.M.

I recognized the voice immediately. It was Fred, a guy I knew in Congressman Dellams's office. His twin girls went to school with my daughter and, last I heard, they'd both joined the Acorn track team.

"John." He sounded shaky and upset.

At once I asked, "What's up?"

"Man, we've got a big problem here," Fred said. "You know Darrell Hampton, the director down at Acorn?"

"Sure." Everyone in the area knew Darrell. He was constantly being feted for one thing or another.

Fred was losing the battle to control his anger. "Some cops beat the holy hell out of him this afternoon, right in front of the kids. He's down at Washington Street. I don't know if he's been arrested or not. Can you go over there? I'd really appreciate it, and so would the congressman."

"You know the cops?" I asked.

"Someone said a guy named Yoell. I don't know the others."

"I'm on my way," I said, grabbing my jacket.

It was eight o'clock before I got in to see Darrell, who was still sitting on a cot in the holding cell. Damn! I had to suck in my breath hard so I wouldn't gasp with horror. Darrell's handsome face was barely recognizable. It was swollen, purple, cracked-looking. The residue of dried blood rimmed his mouth. His clothes were torn and bloody. It *hurt* to look at him.

The guard opened the door to the holding cell. I went in and sat down beside Darrell. "Did they read you your Miranda rights?" He nodded.

"Okay, here's what's happening. You're going to be arraigned in court tomorrow on three counts—possession of a deadly weapon, assaulting a police officer with a weapon, and resisting arrest."

Darrell started to react, then winced. It hurt too much to move the muscles in his face. I held up my hand. "I know. I've read the report. Believe me, there are plenty of folks outside who have a somewhat different view. I have an investigator on his way to interview people."

Darrell stared down at the floor and looked so miserable I wanted to hug him. This must have seemed utterly surreal to him. I put my hand on his shoulder. "The important thing now is to get a doctor in here to look at you. They're going to take some pictures, too, then they'll move you to a regular cell and you can get some sleep. I'll be back at nine tomorrow morning."

"You know what's really crazy about the whole thing?" Darrell said, suddenly. "I was 'Mr. Police.' Sometimes kids would come up to me and complain that they'd been arrested for doing nothing. They'd say, 'Oh, man, they beat me down, they took me to jail, they grabbed me, for no reason.' I'd always tell them the same thing: 'If you weren't doing anything incorrect, that wouldn't have happened. Cops don't do that.' " He slumped down, and his eyes were bright with tears. "I guess I got my wake-up call. What am I going to tell my kids now, Mr. Burris?"

I didn't have an answer.

When I arrived at the courtroom the next morning, it was packed. Everyone was there for Darrell. There were men and women in business suits, elderly people with canes and walkers, young men and women with angry, frightened faces. And there were kids—dozens of kids, as young as five years old. I saw Fred's daughter sitting with a group of girls—the track team, I guessed.

It was a moving sight. I could tell even the DA and the judge were impressed. Darrell still looked like hell when they brought him in, and the crowd in the courtroom rose to its feet and started cheering until the judge finally hammered his gavel and demanded silence.

The counts were read, and Darrell answered, "Not guilty," through his swollen lips. Then he was taken back to his jail cell where he sat for the next two days, fighting the pain and thinking about how his life might be over.

On the third day, I finally got him released on his own recognizance. A court date was set. I met Darrell at the police station, and he hobbled alongside me out to the curb where I was double-parked. "Get in," I said, opening the car door. "We're taking you to the hospital."

The charges against Darrell were later dropped without explanation. It wasn't hard to figure out why. In the coming months, I worked with Darrell on a civil case against the officers and the police department. By now I was familiar with the catalog of injuries he had sustained: a dislocated jaw, a cut and swollen lip, facial lacerations and bruises, a wrenched neck and partially crushed larynx, contusions to the neck and ribs, and cuts and scrapes on his knees and legs. There was nerve damage in his lower back and neck, for which he was going to physical therapy three times a week.

While we were preparing our case, we received a ruling

from OPD Internal Affairs: Proof of brutality not sustained against Officers Boyovich, Johnson, and Woods. Proof of brutality sustained against Yoell.

A victory? Not really. Yoell's punishment was a thirty-day suspension. Thirty lousy days, after a career of misconduct.

One afternoon, I drove over to the Acorn project. It was late and the community center was closed for the day. A young boy who looked to be about thirteen sat slumped on the bottom step, idly kicking pebbles across the asphalt. He looked up at me with deliberate indifference. I thought to myself: psychic numbing.

I held out a hand. "I'm John Burris," I said.

He didn't move. Just looked down at the ground. "That lawyer," he said flatly.

"Yeah." I sat next to him on the step. "What's your name?"

"Reggie."

"Reggie, did you see what happened to Darrell?"

"Yeah." He shrugged as if it didn't matter. "No use talking about it. Can't do nothing."

I felt a stab of rage to see a boy of thirteen already entrenched in his hopelessness. I knew too well where this could lead: drugs, violence—and the same kind of cold brutality he had witnessed from the cops. It grieved me that people could ask, "How do we stop the cycle of violence?" Wasn't it clear?

Before Reggie had joined the Acorn Community Center, he had been starting to head in the wrong direction. He thought of himself as a tough kid. He got into a lot of fights. He was disrespectful of authority. One day, Darrell had glanced out the window of the center and saw a police officer approach

Reggie in the courtyard. Darrell didn't know Reggie, but he could see that the kid had an attitude; he was being a little mouthy. Suddenly the cop hit the kid hard in the face, sending him sprawling. Then the cop walked away.

After that, Darrell made it a point to get to know Reggie. It wasn't easy to break through his hard shell, but after a little more than a year he had succeeded. Reggie became one of Darrell's brightest kids. He got involved with the Police Athletic League and DARE. He became convinced that Darrell was right: The cops were okay. Maybe Reggie would be a cop someday.

Reggie suddenly balled up his fists and said fiercely, "I know cops beat up people for no reason. I wish cops were regular people so I could go beat *them* up for what they did to Darrell."

He was a tough guy again—but there were tears in his eyes.

Darrell's case was strong. I felt confident that I could win a measure of justice for him in civil court. But I knew I couldn't achieve justice for the children. There isn't a court in the nation that would define the trauma those kids experienced as abuse. And *that's* what kept me awake at night.

What children see in ten minutes of police brutality changes them for life. For older kids like Reggie, in whom Darrell carefully nurtured the beginnings of trust and optimism, it causes a rift in their relationship with the law enforcement community that might never be repaired. For younger children, like Elsie and Pooter, it snaps the barely formed tendrils of their faith in the world. They never again feel safe. Even their heroes can't protect them.

Many of the children were traumatized enough to need

therapy after the incident. Some had nightmares; others cried whenever they saw a police officer walk through the project. Their carefree landscape had shifted; everything seemed colored with danger now.

The OPD settled the suit for $225,000 before it went to trial. I insisted, as a part of the settlement, that $5,000 come out of Yoell's pocket. I wanted him to experience some personal accountability. It's too easy for cops to walk away from their responsibility when the department foots the bill. This was sending a message to Michael Yoell: There are consequences.

SAVING THE CHILDREN

The Acorn Community Center closed. The entire project is being torn down to erect condominiums. I've stayed in touch with Darrell over the years. He's continued to work with youths in the community. His track team won the national championship in 1997.

A chain-link fence surrounds the old project now, as construction goes on. On one day, Darrell and I stand there and watch the workmen demolish the community center. Large concrete slabs, pulled from the building, are piled in the yard where children once played. The leaden jaws of huge cranes tear at the facade.

Today Darrell possesses a hardness that wasn't there in 1990—or maybe he's just more realistic. He is not a bitter man. His greatest regret is for the kids who had their trust shattered, and for the victories dampened by the atmosphere of defeat. The year of the incident, Darrell's girls' track team won the high-school state championship—the first time an Oakland team had ever done so. What should have been a moment of tremendous pride and joy, was bitter. "It was hard for the kids to have their coach being portrayed by cops as an evil, pool cue–slingin' guy," Darrell tells me. "It was hard for me, too. My team had just won the championship, and who was I? I was the brother who got jumped by the police."

Darrell points to his chest and says, "Here, inside, it changed me. I have to be more careful now—think about how I can be a role model and still let kids know they've got to be careful. I used to say, 'You've got to believe in something. You've got to trust someone. So trust in the badge.' I don't say that anymore."

While we're standing there at the site of the demolished project, Darrell mentions something else, though, that represents hope. "My track-and-field team has a 100-percent high-school graduation rate," he says proudly, "and a 100-percent college acceptance rate. Sixteen of my girls are in college right now. That's my goal with kids—achievement, excellence, education."

So, that's the whole of it. Some kids are scarred and never get past it. Some kids are scarred and rise above it. And Darrell keeps working toward the time when there are no more scars.

Chapter 5

THE FOX
IN THE
HENHOUSE

We cannot live by power, and a culture that seeks to live by it becomes brutal and sterile.

—MAX LERNER

What is most disturbing about Darrell's case is that cops like Yoell and Boyovich had such extensive records of brutality. Where was the red flag, the early-warning system that would have taken them off the street before this incident could occur? Where was the judgment from superior officers that Mike Yoell was exactly the kind of cop who would speed through a playground filled with young children at 30 miles an hour; a cop who would discard the obvious fact of Darrell's intentions; a cop who would bristle dangerously when he was challenged in any way?

In the grand scheme of things, officers like Yoell and Boyovich represent a small percentage of the police force, but the damage they do far exceeds their numbers. They are like a deadly poison; a single drop can infect their entire environment.

The question of how to weed out the few bad cops has been the subject of endless review and countless recommendations on a local and national level. But the question of who can effectively judge the police has never been fruitfully answered. Instead it has remained a paradox, grounded in a fundamental attitude of distrust between the police and the communities they serve. Traditionally police departments have thrived on an air of secrecy when it comes to their policies and practices.

A high-ranking officer once explained to me, "People may see a police officer engaging in what they consider unfair or abusive behavior, and think, *That's wrong.* But they're not *us.* They don't know any of the background, they don't understand departmental policy, and they don't have any idea what an officer sees and reacts to, or what he's supposed to do."

Considering the enormous stresses police officers may be placed under at any time, and the diverse elements of society that we ask them to deal with and regulate on a daily basis, I do agree up to a point that citizens cannot always evaluate situations fairly and knowledgeably. However, in most police misconduct cases, the issue at hand is whether or not a citizen's constitutional rights have been violated, and this is a fairly objective standard. We do not tell our police officers that the end justifies the means, that they are allowed to step outside the law in order to enforce it.

Police departments themselves are incapable of being the sole judges of the behavior of officers, for the simple reason that they exist as a fraternity apart from society. Internal Affairs is not an independent investigative body. There's a built-in bias in favor of the officer.

There are countless examples of citizens' complaints being ruled "unsustained" (meaning there wasn't enough proof), or "unfounded" (meaning it never happened), by Internal Affairs departments. The internal police disciplinary process has frustrated citizens, and led to the sentiment that "the foxes are guarding the henhouse."

In recent years, civilian review boards have been formed in many cities to provide a forum for accountability by the police. However, they too, have been subject to a host of problems, including political agendas, hack appointments, and an ultimate lack of any legitimate authority or power.

The vast majority of civilian complaint review boards can write as many reports and make as many recommendations as they wish to the mayor and the police commissioner. They can publish their findings and have them disseminated on radio and television—it won't matter. Their influence is often hollow because they are not the final decision-makers.

A "FAMILY" AFFAIR

Police departments would prefer that all complaints against police officers be handled by their own Internal Affairs Division—kind of like not airing dirty laundry for the neighbors to see.

Their argument is that trained and experienced law-enforcement officers understand better than laypersons what police officers are trained to do in given circumstances. Furthermore, police departments tend to distrust the community's ability (especially a minority community) to judge an officer's actions fairly and without prejudice.

However, Internal Affairs investigations offer little opportunity for the complainant to be heard. Invariably, when it's his or her word against a police officer's, the complaint is judged "unfounded"—even when the officer in question has a history of misconduct or abuse complaints.

And, even when Internal Affairs "sustains" a complaint, the sanctions often fall painfully short of being reasonable—or punitive.

Darrell Hampton's complaint is a case in point. It was not sustained against Boyovich, Johnson, and Woods; and while it *was* sustained against Yoell, he received only a thirty-day suspension before he was returned to the street. He was later promoted to sergeant. The department ignored the fox in its own henhouse. A man like Yoell was not merely guilty of poor judgment, failure to follow departmental policy, and overreacting to an incident. His history and style of violence clearly indicated a fundamental disrespect for the people he served.

Similar scenarios are repeated in many cities. An examination of Internal Affairs investigations in the Philadelphia Police Department found that the vast majority of more than *two thousand* citizen complaints between 1989 and 1998, led nowhere. There were occasional suspensions handed out for especially egregious misconduct, but the process of punishing officers was so complex and labyrinthine that, as a department supervisor explained, "even *we* have trouble figuring it out."

I am not suggesting that every complaint against a police officer has merit. Clearly, many do not. People lie to get off the hook; they lie to get back at an officer who may have arrested them, or a friend, or a family member; they overreact; they resist a legitimate arrest and cause the actions that take place. But it's ludicrous to believe that 84 percent of citizen complaints are unwarranted—as Philadelphia's records suggests.

As a recent *Dateline NBC* demonstrated, it can be difficult for a citizen to file a complaint with Internal Affairs. *Dateline* sent an undercover reporter into several precincts in New York City. In each case, the reporter posed as a black citizen who told the desk officer he wanted to file a complaint against an officer. In all but one precinct, the reporter was treated with hostility, asked, "What did *you* do?" in a sarcastic manner, and refused a complaint form until he was first interviewed about the incident. One precinct did it right. The desk officer gave him a form and politely explained how to fill it out.

Can you imagine how intimidating it can be to walk into a police station and announce that you want to file a complaint? And even when you succeed in doing so, you are rarely, if ever, informed of how Internal Affairs reaches its final decision. A curt letter is all you receive.

Several years ago, I represented an elderly woman who was treated so dismissively by Internal Affairs that it infuriated me.

"PRECIOUS"

Bertha Ketter was a frail woman in her late sixties, who looked at least ten years older. She had lived in West Oakland for most of her adult life. In a community where gangs and drugs flourish, it was a source of great pride to her that she had been able to raise her children well; none of them had ever been in trouble with the law. Bertha was a well-known figure in the community, a property owner, and someone who helped people out.

On October 30, 1992, Bertha was walking down the street with Carl, a handyman, who was helping her move some boxes to her property.

Bertha and Carl were standing at the corner, waiting for the light to change, when a car pulled up in front of them, blocking their path. Officer Williams, a black female officer jumped out and yelled, "Get back on the curb!" Bertha backed up. Officer Williams ran up to her and placed strong hands tightly around her throat, yelling "Spit it out!"—while choking her.

At the same time, a second officer, T. K. Lewis, a white male officer, moved over to Bertha, grabbing her by the nose and squeezing. Lewis yelled, "Spit it out, Precious!"

Precious was the name of a woman who bore no resemblance to Bertha, except for being black. Precious allegedly ran a crack house in the area, and Officer Lewis hadn't seen Precious in six years, and never on the street.

Meanwhile Bertha was choking, and her small body was rigid with fear. Carl was shouting, "Her name is not Precious!"

"Shut the fuck up!" yelled Officer Lewis.

After a couple of minutes of this, Bertha gagged and spit out her chewing gum, followed by her upper dentures. Officer Lewis, finding no drugs in Bertha's mouth, began to unbutton her sweater, causing her to raise her arms protectively around her chest. Carl advised Bertha to cooperate with the officers, hoping they would eventually leave her alone. Bertha lowered her arms, and Officer Lewis frisked her.

Finally, finding no evidence of crack, Officer Williams released her chokehold, and the two cops, without another word, got into their car and drove away.

Bertha Ketter stood there, badly shaken up, humiliated, and in pain from the choking she'd received.

As any normal person would, Bertha felt that something should be done, so later, accompanied by her son, she went down to the station to file a formal complaint with Internal Affairs.

After she described what had happened, the IA officer asked her if she went by another name. She said no. She was then asked to remove her coat and expose her arms. "Are you a drug user?" he asked.

Bertha was shocked. "No!" she replied indignantly. How could he even suggest that?

The officer had photos taken of her neck and profile, and that was it. Before Bertha left, she asked the officer for a written and verbal apology—which was all she really wanted—but was told that would be impossible.

At home, while lying down to rest, Ketter started to experience trouble swallowing. She was taken by her son to the hospital where the attending doctor told her that she had deep bruises which penetrated to the inside of her throat. She was treated and given medication.

Some time later, Bertha received a formal notice from Internal Affairs, stating that the department had found her complaint "unfounded." In other words, it never happened. Bertha was outraged. All she had asked for was a simple apology, a little show of respect.

She didn't want to sue, but she finally did, and I easily won a settlement for her from the department. Part of the settlement—the most important part to Bertha—was that she would receive a letter of apology from the department.

A CLOSED SOCIETY

The secrecy that surrounds internal police investigations naturally engenders distrust in the community. Citizens aren't usually notified if any disciplinary action has been taken in a complaint case. And if any has been taken, and they find out what it is, the almost universal response is, "That's all?" Ten days', fifteen days', thirty days' suspension. An occasional fine. It doesn't seem like enough. In New York City, when an officer is punished after a hearing, a city law limits penalties—short of dismissal—to a month's suspension and a year's departmental probation.

There are so many layers of appeal that even when an officer is sanctioned or dismissed, the union steps in and often gets the judgment reversed. In 1997, Philadelphia's Internal Affairs Division decided that, out of approximately 400 citizen complaints, 66 were legitimate—one in six. The majority of officers involved in the 66 sustained complaints appealed to the Police Board of Inquiry, a panel of three officers, all union members. The board reversed the Internal Affairs ruling in 12 of the 66 cases, and exonerated the officers involved.

If officers lost their cases, they had a union right to arbitration, even if the police commissioner had suspended or fired them. The Philadelphia solicitor's office defends the police commissioner's actions at the arbitration hearing against the union lawyer. The city solicitor's office sends a paralegal, rather than an attorney, to the hearing. Arbitration regulations have made the police commissioner unable to maintain any meaningful discipline among his officers. No matter what he does, the case goes to arbitration, and usually the officer in question goes back to work.

City councilman Michael Nutter told the *Philadelphia Inquirer*, "The arbitration system is in serious need of examination and repair. There are officers the police department got rid of and does not want, and they are out there with a badge and gun."

There's also the concern that complaints handled internally by the police will take a speedy trip to a shredder. Outsiders have very little access to police investigation files. Recently, in New York City, it was discovered that a conspiracy to "lose" complaints against 108 cops had been under way for some time. Complaints that had been substantiated and sustained by the civilian Complaint Review Board between 1993 and 1995 were "lost" before they could be forwarded to the New York City Police Department for disciplinary action.

Lack of access to records is a big problem. Even Amnesty International ran into a blue wall when it attempted to investigate 15 deaths in police custody in New York City between 1988 and 1995, most of which happened on the streets.

The causes of death varied from asphyxia from pressure on the neck and chest, to signs of having been struck. A number of the deaths occurred during violent struggles with the police. Two prisoners in custody in 1995 died from ingesting too much pepper spray, a chemical agent used to disable a person. From 1990 to 1994, *89 percent* of those who died while in the custody of the New York City Police Department were African-American or Hispanic. Amnesty International claimed that those figures by themselves were disturbing, and warranted an independent inquiry.

However, under New York State law, police internal disciplinary reports are confidential, as are the findings of the CCRB. The authorities did not respond to Amnesty International's questions as to whether or not internal disciplinary action had been taken against officers in certain cases.

John Hoffman, a citizen who has sued the Seattle Police Department for lack of access to documents, discovered that they'd go to great lengths to limit his ability to gain access. On the few records he did receive, they blacked out the parts that contained critical information, much as people discovered when they saw long-hidden FBI files released under the Freedom of Information Act.

At least 136 documents John Hoffman claims to have requested were presumably destroyed by the Seattle Police Department as part of their "routine deletion of such files after they are three years old." Hoffman had requested them before they were destroyed, and other records he received contained large gaps and missing pages.

BIAS FROM WITHIN

But, as always, there's another side to the equation, and in this case, it's the officer's. The way the disciplinary system works in many departments is that any officer accused of misconduct goes through a hearing process and a review of the complaint, which may take weeks or even months. If a shooting is involved, the officer is taken out of the field and placed on "modified duty," which usually means working at a desk, until the case comes up for a hearing. Many officers feel that their careers will be permanently damaged if they're even placed in the position of being taken out of the regular rotation for such an extended period of time. And, since most hearings end with the officer cleared completely of any wrongdoing, it's considered an unfair process.

Despite this system, which gives them every benefit, officers still believe that the results of the hearings are too random, that what may bring one officer up on a charge, will get another officer a commendation, or even a promotion in rank. There are no official guidelines as to penalties.

Police administrators counter by noting that each case must be judged and examined on its own, as a case separate from any other, and therefore subject to varying penalties at the pleasure of the police commissioner or chief.

Still, the internal disciplinary process can be unfair, even discriminatory, depending upon who's in charge, and how each case of misconduct or abuse of police power is gauged and then acted upon.

For instance, figures filed in early 1998 with the Federal Equal Employment Opportunity Commission by the Latino

Officers' Association, showed that female, black, and Latino officers were twice as likely as white male officers to be brought up on departmental charges—no matter where they worked. What conclusions are to be drawn? Do women and minority groups make less effective police officers than do white males? Or are they prone to misconduct and abuse even more so than their white male counterparts?

None of the above. It's obvious that the same bludgeon used against females, blacks, and Hispanics when they initially integrated the nation's police forces is still being wielded.

TRACKING ROGUE COPS

I have always been puzzled that so little effort has been made to monitor the few police officers in every department who receive frequent complaints. In Oakland, I have repeatedly encountered the same cops in civil cases involving brutality; there was one officer who was the subject of 37 investigations before he eventually left the force.

In nearly every city police force I studied, I found examples of the same unchecked brutality. Often it takes a widely publicized case before an officer with a history of violence is noted.

In New Orleans, a police officer known in the black community as "Robocop," because of his cold manner and heavy-handed abuse, was finally stopped when he was caught on tape, ordering the murder of a woman who had filed a brutality complaint against him, and later speaking approvingly of the murder after it was committed. Records revealed that in a period of five years, this officer was the subject of more than twenty complaints, most involving brutality and physical intimidation. An officer in the department was quoted as saying, "He's got an Internal Affairs jacket as thick as a telephone book, but supervisors have swept his dirt under the rug for so long that it's coming back to haunt them."

In November 1996, the police officer was sentenced to death for the murder of the woman. It is a terrible tragedy that he wasn't stopped sooner.

There is an element of denial involved in the failure to identify and eliminate brutal cops from the force. Whenever a highly publicized case occurs, police departments and city governments scramble to get the message out that it is an isolated incident.

In August 1997, after Abner Louima, a Haitian immigrant, was tortured and sodomized with a toilet plunger inside a Brooklyn police station, Mayor Rudy Giuliani and Police Commissioner Howard Safir immediately held a press conference to condemn the officers involved, and to order a full-scale investigation. However, they refused to give weight to reports that the precinct itself was a hotbed of abuse, and the commissioner went so far as to say that the attack against Louima was not police brutality, it was a crime. This peculiar reasoning would lead one to believe that the commissioner does not consider "ordinary" police brutality to be criminal.

I've heard notorious incidents of police brutality called "isolated incidents" countless times, but we all know that they are not isolated. To call them such is an insult to the truth, and a serious form of denial.

For a positive result to emerge from such a terrible incident, we must look deeper than the specifics of a single case and acknowledge the existence of an ongoing problem. That's the key. Not just accountability for the behavior of individual cops, but accountability for the culture that condones brutality and even encourages police to show disrespect to the community they are charged to protect.

WHEN CITIZENS HAVE A SAY

Some form of a citizen review board now exists in at least one hundred U.S. cities, but to date, the results have been disappointing. Citizen boards are plagued by inaction, and are not ordinarily empowered by any real authority. In fact, they are often so meaningless that their existence barely registers on the radar screen. In 1995, in the aftermath of an incident involving a police officer's shooting of an innocent citizen, the mayor of Atlanta responded to community outrage by calling for the creation of a civilian review board—only to be informed that one already existed.

The reasons for inaction by citizen review boards are many and varied. Sometimes the makeup of the board is politically motivated or left to the discretion of the police commissioner—automatically tainting its objectivity. Often, citizen review boards don't have access to certain information about an officer, and their recommendations have no power to override Internal Affairs decisions.

A persistent complaint about citizen review boards is that

their record of acknowledging the validity of civilian complaints is often no better than Internal Affairs—in other words—that they are nothing more than an arm of the police department. A recent review of the New York City Civilian Complaint Review Board, established in the wake of the Mollen Report, found that between July 1993 and December 1996, only *4 percent* of the 16,327 complaints were found by the commission to have merit, and only *1 percent* resulted in disciplinary action against police officers. Most telling was the statistic that more than 80 percent of the incidents that generated complaints were not made in the context of arrests or summonses, but by law-abiding citizens who had encounters with police officers.

Citizen complaint boards frequently grouse that they are not equipped to do the investigative work that would truly make them independent. The Citizens' Police Complaint Office in Indianapolis is typical. The office is poorly funded and has no investigators of its own, forcing it to rely on investigations conducted by the police.

Funding was also an issue with the Washington, D.C., Civilian Complaint Review Board—to the extent that the board was abolished in 1995. A powerful police union that lobbied against the board tied its hands even further. Since 1995, various proposals have been floated by the police department and the city council, but one of the most recent underscores the lack of commitment to a truly independent board. The city council suggested the creation of an external review board, using police officers as investigators and retired judges as the review panel. Frustrated by the lack of acceptable proposals, an independent task force was created by city activists in 1997. To date, however, there remains no independent review structure.

Los Angeles has no independent citizens' review mechanism, and the Christopher Commission did not recommend one. Instead, the city has a civilian oversight committee called the Police Commission. However, its role is bolstered by a newly created Office of the Inspector General, whose sole purpose is to track the progress being made toward implementing the Christopher Commission's recommendations. A report is published every six months—and so far, these reports have been refreshingly frank.

WHAT WORKS?

According to Sam Walker, a University of Nebraska criminal-justice professor who studies the effectiveness of review boards, in cities where these boards work, "public faith in the ability of police to police themselves increases.

"The most effective panels are those that have the power to investigate allegations of the police misconduct, without having to rely on information gained in prior investigations by police," Walker says. "The least effective are the ones that simply duplicate work. The ones that don't work are the ones with no vision."

Even activist cities, such as San Francisco, struggle to build an effective coalition between the police and the community. The police department in San Francisco is supervised by a civilian Police Commission. Civilian complaints of police abuse aren't investigated by the department. Instead, separate investigators working for the Office of Citizen Complaints— *not the police*—look into the matter.

However, according to a 1996 investigative report by the *San Francisco Examiner*, the city was paying out large awards in civil lawsuits following officer-involved shootings, but the officers were escaping punishment by the police department, receiving no discipline and being shielded from criminal prosecution.

The *Examiner* investigation revealed that between 1990 and 1995, police involvement in shooting deaths averaged 4.1 people per every 100 murders committed, a higher rate of involvement than Los Angeles, New York, or Oakland. The *Examiner* also revealed that 75 percent of the people shot or killed by the police between 1993 and 1996 were minorities, or people living in low-income neighborhoods.

In the city election that took place in November 1995, Proposition G was passed by the voters of San Francisco. Among its many statutes, one requires that the police department's budget must pay for all settlements of civil cases brought because of police misconduct. The idea is to force the department to track problem officers, and focus on retraining or disciplining them properly, especially those who cost the department the funds necessary to operate at its peak efficiency. Since the city isn't allowed to let its police-department capabilities fall below a certain level, Proposition G promises to add more accountability to the department. In fact, a new position of "risk manager" has been created within the department to oversee and respond to civilian complaints against the police.

San Francisco's citizenry has made it so difficult for the police that the vice president of the police union has been quoted as saying that this is "without a doubt, the most difficult city in America to be a cop. Cops are finally saying, 'You know what? I've had it!' "

Portland, Oregon, which doesn't have a citizen review board, has established a well-organized watchdog effort, called Copwatch, to monitor the police. The goal of Copwatch is to promote police accountability through citizen action. Copwatch takes reports, and presents complainants with options to seek remands in cases of police misconduct, harassment, and/or brutality.

JUSTICE FOR VICTIMS

It has been my experience that victims of police brutality want to see the officers punished. For them, justice is not completed with a check from the department for their pain and suffering. Victims usually want the police officers to be fired or placed in a position where they can never brutalize anyone again. Unfortunately, the system is not designed for that to occur, except in the most egregious circumstances.

In the early 1990s there was an incident in New York City involving a homeless man who had been beaten by police. Although the man's civil-rights lawyer, James I. Meyerson, secured a settlement of $200,000 for his client, the homeless man was not satisfied. He wanted the officers who'd hurt him punished.

So Meyerson filed a second suit, demanding that the city discipline the officers involved. They had lost nothing in terms of wages or even vacation days for an incident which cost the city $200,000. The lawsuit was dismissed.

Was this an isolated incident? Of course not. Police misconduct cases are reported far less often than the incidents themselves occur, and, of those that are reported, few are brought to the level of a court trial.

Chapter 6

WALKING WHILE BLACK

Am I not a man and a brother?
—Inscription on the seal of the
Antislavery Society, 1770

Walking home from the Lucky Supermarket one night, Doug Stevens was in a good mood. He had a very pretty lady coming over to his place later, and he was looking forward to her company. As he ambled down the street, the bustle of his busy East Oakland neighborhood was friendly and familiar.

Doug Stevens—a concerned citizen: "I know firsthand."

Doug's neighborhood was just like so many others in Oakland—single-story, working-class homes and small apartment buildings. Pride was evident in the lovingly cared-for plots of land, tiny squares of green brimming with flower beds, neatly painted houses behind white picket fences. The residents knew one another and felt a protective bond.

However, late most nights, you'd find groups of kids standing on various corners, at first glance indistinguishable from guys like Doug. But, on closer scrutiny, you'd see they were dealers—polluting a law-abiding community with their merchandise and their presence.

The popular misconception is that drugs are found and sold only in infamous "bad neighborhoods," but Oakland often finds its drug dealers in the heart of respectable working-class neighborhoods. Unfortunately, police officers don't always attempt to make the distinction. The officers who encountered Doug that night didn't bother to see if he was actually one of the bad guys or not. With the same respect they'd show a hardened hood, the officers plucked Doug off the street, effectively canceling his plans for the evening.

Doug Stevens was a tall and muscular young man who lifted weights at the gym. But his imposing physique belied his manner, which was gentle, soft-spoken, and community-minded. Enrolled at the local community college, he had made friends with those who were active politically. One of these college friends, Dwayne Hall, was on the student council, and shared Stevens's interest in the problems in the community—notably, regarding the regular incidents of overaggressive behavior by the police toward young men in the neighborhood. Walking down the street, you were liable to see somebody you knew detained by the police, up against the wall, his arms spread. Doug had expressed to Dwayne an interest in taking part in the student council, to do what he could.

Earlier that evening Doug had briefly visited Dwayne's apartment. He was in a gregarious mood, laughing and chatting as he drank Kool-Aid. The young woman who was joining him for dinner later—a beautiful girl, a model—had been the object of young Stevens's attentions for some time, and he was elated when she finally accepted his invitation. This evening was his chance to win her over, and everything had to be perfect. He had planned on cooking her a pasta dinner, his specialty.

Doug was handsomely turned out, in a nice pair of slacks, polished shoes, and a trench coat when he began walking the five blocks to the supermarket to shop for dinner. He made his purchases and started back, his step a little jauntier than usual, out of anticipation of the evening ahead. Around the corner from his apartment, he stopped to chew the fat with a small group of teenagers, boys and girls, two white plastic shopping bags in his hands.

Suddenly a police cruiser, driven by Officer Ricardo Orozco, pulled up alongside them and screeched to a stop. Officer Orozco was a young cop. Twenty-six years old, he'd only been on the force for a couple of years, doing patrol duty. Orozco had received a call over his car radio about a disturbance in the neighborhood. It was a nonspecific call. No actual disturbance was ever found, and it was never discovered who made the call.

Officer Orozco had been driving around, had spotted Doug Stevens and the kids, and made an intuitive leap—the wrong intuitive leap, an assumption. Although nothing was going on that could even remotely be called horseplay, he decided that this was the site of the disturbance that had been called out over his radio.

Later, Orozco would report that he hadn't noticed any girls—although girls *were* there. He recalled seeing only Stevens and a group of boys. The implication formed in his mind that they were drug dealers, and that the well-dressed Stevens was their leader. Orozco leaned out his driver's-side window, and called to Stevens, "Let me see some identification!"

Stevens, taken by surprise at this sudden turn of events— the abrupt end of his free and easy mood—shrugged and replied, "I haven't got any, Officer. I lost my wallet."

A police officer has the right to ask a citizen to show identification. He also has the right to detain the citizen if the citizen cannot produce it. However, training, discretion, and common sense would dictate that being aggressive wasn't necessary. Perhaps a more experienced or more sensitive officer might have pulled alongside the group and casually asked Stevens what was up. He might have mentioned that there had been a report of a disturbance. He might also have evaluated the scene for a moment before he became belligerent. There was nothing in the demeanor of Stevens or any of the youths that would send up a red flag—unless, of course, you assume that young blacks in a group automatically represent some kind of a danger or threat.

When Stevens, still holding the plastic grocery bags in both hands, told Officer Orozco that he didn't have identification,

Orozco jumped out of his cruiser and ran at Stevens, yelling, "Put your fucking hands behind your head!"

Confused, Stevens responded, "What did I do? Can I just put down my groceries?" The cop seemed agitated. Stevens repeated himself a few times—"What did I do?" As the officer tried grabbing Stevens's huge arms and bringing them behind his back, he kept telling Stevens to put his hands up. As the physical impossibility of this order became apparent to Officer Orozco, he became even more agitated.

Hasha Foley, a woman who lived in a house with a window looking out on the street, would later testify that she hadn't heard any disturbance preceding the incident with the officer, but was prompted to her window by the frantic cry of Doug Stevens imploring, "What did I do? What did I do?"

As Hasha Foley watched the scene unfold below, she thought, *This guy better do what this cop says. He's getting mad.* She was suddenly afraid for Stevens. *Why doesn't he just put his hands up?* she wondered.

In the street below, Orozco was trying to put handcuffs on Stevens, and Stevens was resisting. He hadn't done anything. Could you just be arrested for standing on the sidewalk? He felt he had a right to know what the charges were.

Orozco hit Stevens on the head with his flashlight. It was one of those long, heavy-duty, mostly solid metal flashlights that takes four D batteries and weighs several pounds, more or less. The flashlight struck Stevens on the left temple, and the bags flew out of his hands. The groceries rolled down the pavement. The group of kids that had been hanging out, took off while they had the chance, and disappeared.

Stunned and scared, Stevens thought, *This guy's crazy!* He was going to get beat up if he didn't do something. What could he do? He held his head with his hand where the blow had landed.

"Did anybody see that?" he yelled reflexively. Dazed, ignoring Orozco, and noticing his groceries all over the street, he leaned over to pick them up and put them back in the bags.

But Officer Orozco wasn't done with Doug Stevens yet. He then grabbed him by the arms and struggled to get control of Stevens.

"Why are you doing this?" Stevens asked, his voice a sob. "What did I do?" Officer Orozco had put away the flashlight and now was wielding a large baton in his hand. Still giving no explanation to Stevens, he started to hit him on his flanks with the nightstick. Stevens didn't even try to defend himself by striking back at Orozco. Orozco was hurting Stevens, and Doug knew he'd better just go along before this guy killed him.

Stunned, but now complying with Officer Orozco, Stevens let himself be led to the front hood of the police car, with Orozco holding his hands tightly behind his back. Orozco pressed him to take the spread position on the front hood. At this point, a second police car screeched to a halt behind Orozco's. Out leapt Officer Monica Russo, a short but solid female cop. Without pausing to ask any questions, Russo jumped up onto the hood and put Stevens in a headlock, saying to him, "You've got a fucking problem?" Once she had a good grip around Stevens's neck she jumped off the hood, causing Stevens to fall straight back on the ground, with

Russo's full weight landing on top of him. With the help of Orozco, she got up and turned him over onto his stomach to handcuff him.

When police officers are called as backup, they are expected to act quickly when they arrive on the scene. At the same time, their training should allow them to instantly evaluate the level of danger. Stevens was spread on the front hood when Russo arrived. He wasn't fighting. The situation was under control. Her subsequent actions were baffling and completely without reason.

Around this time, Dwayne Hall, who had been with Doug just before he had gone to the supermarket, was about to leave his building to go over to Doug's apartment, when the building's superintendent warned him to be careful because there were a lot of police cars on the street. Hall walked outside only to see his friend Doug on the ground, surrounded by cops, his groceries in a heap, cans rolling down the sidewalk.

"It was really a mindblower," he said later, in a deposition, "because we were always talking about that kind of stuff going on in the community." Doug, of all people, getting beaten by the police! In vain, Dwayne Hall ran to get help. He would later testify for Stevens as a witness to the beating.

In any case, Stevens wasn't going anywhere. He wasn't doing anything. The impact of the fall and the whole absurd shock of the situation, was getting to Stevens. Dizzy, dazed, and in pain, he lay on the ground, surrounded by a growing corps of police cruisers, flashing lights, and blue uniforms. As if he were in a surreal dream, he could hear himself faintly from a long distance off, screaming for them to leave him alone, shouting that they didn't need to do this to him, crying for them to let him go.

But Doug Stevens's nightmare didn't end there. Once he'd been handcuffed, various officers started beating him with their nightsticks, kicking him in the head, stomping on his legs.

From her window, Hasha Foley started yelling, "Hey, this is getting out of hand!" *They're going to break this guy's legs,* she thought. But the police seemed oblivious—focused like dogs on a bone. Stevens was helpless. He was yelling, "Help! Help!" The only response to his cries was the sound of laughter and excited chatter among the officers. Hasha Foley was disgusted. She turned to a friend visiting her. "Listen. Did you hear that? They're bragging about it!"

On the ground, Stevens wasn't thinking clearly, but he was *feeling.* He was helpless. Humiliated. Here he was, a big guy who took pride in his body—over six feet tall, two hundred forty pounds of muscle—and he was getting the stuffing beaten out of him, making him cry out in pain, helpless in front of people he passed by on the street every day. Why was this happening? He hadn't been violent. He hadn't given the officers any reason to hit him.

At some point, the officers laid off and finally stopped altogether. One of them picked up Stevens by his handcuffs and threw him, aching, a large gash on his forehead, into a paddy wagon. Once inside, by this time starting to really hurt from the beating he'd taken, Stevens asked the cops in front to take him to the hospital. They told him to shut up and sit down, while they joked around, smoking cigarettes. Stevens sat on the hard bench of the wagon, handcuffed and badly injured, as it made its regular rounds, picking up other waiting detainees until there were fourteen of them packed in the back.

More than an hour had gone by before they stopped at Highland Hospital, where Orozco took Stevens inside and had him looked at. Although Orozco would later write on his report that Stevens was intoxicated, he ordered no blood test. The reason Orozco took Stevens to the hospital was for treatment of injuries the police officers had inflicted. But it didn't really seem to be for Stevens's benefit. After a brief look-over—no dressings or stitches or X rays—he was taken back into the wagon, which drove around another half hour before ending up at the jail. Based on Orozco's report, Stevens was booked on charges of being drunk in public, resisting arrest, and battery on a "peace officer."

Doug Stevens hadn't had any alcohol that evening. He was described by Dwayne Hall as "a big Kool-Aid drinker." He was known as a gregarious fellow. Perhaps, being in a good mood, he or some of the kids raised their voices during their brief conversation on the street. One can only speculate, because nobody seems to have taken notice of Stevens until Officer Orozco arrived.

Stevens spent the next five days and nights in jail. Finally a deputy came to his cell, and he was told that the police had dropped all charges and he was free to go. No explanation. No apologies.

Pulled off the street—beaten, cuffed, beaten some more—five days and five nights locked up. Now you're free to go. Doug Stevens wasn't about to let it go. He felt *wronged.* As he told me later, "There's people like me out there that are getting beaten by the police, and they aren't bringing their cases to trial. They're not taking these officers to court, and so these guys are getting away with it.

"And so I said to myself, 'I'm not gonna be like them. I'm gonna take it to court. I'm gonna stand up. I'm gonna make a difference.' And that's why I went to court, so they wouldn't get away with it."

After being released from the city jail, Stevens returned to the site of the incident to find people who had witnessed what had happened. It wasn't hard. After ringing a couple of doorbells he came upon Hasha Foley, who had seen the whole thing from her window. She agreed to testify on Stevens's behalf, as did his friend Dwayne Hall.

It turned out that the street had been full of witnesses that night. Doug Stevens later learned that people were hollering at the police officers, who ignored them. Some folks had seen this kind of thing—a man being beaten by several police officers—again and again. Younger kids, who were still at an impressionable age, learned a lesson that evening about what the police could do to you if they wanted to. They could take a guy in the middle of a conversation with some friends, a shopping bag of groceries in each hand, knock him to the ground and beat the hell out of him without so much as a by-your-leave. Even a big guy like Doug Stevens, tall and strong. They could do this in front of dozens of witnesses, watching from the windows or just passing by, and get away with it.

My first encounter with Douglas Stevens came not long after he'd been released from his five days in jail. It's typical of my daily life in Oakland that I can't go outside without people coming up to me, telling me they recognize me, asking for legal advice. Most of the time it doesn't bother me. I can lend a moment of my time to say hello, and give them my card. If they have a real need for a lawyer, and I can't help them, I can always refer them to a colleague. No problem, my pleasure. But I met Doug Stevens while I was working out in a health club, sweating away. A friend of mine who works in the club came up to me with him, introduced Stevens, and said he needed my services—he had been beaten up by the cops. At first I was annoyed. I felt like saying, "Hey, guys, I'm trying to work out here! Give me a little space, please!" I told Stevens to come by my office and we'd discuss it, not even expecting him to call. To me he was just some guy in a gym with a story. I didn't know any of the specific details.

He called and made an appointment, and when he came to my office, he was well-dressed and respectful. He told me his story in a soft, compelling voice. I was moved. I could see right away that he was a nice guy, with an affable manner. He had done nothing wrong, and the pain was visible on his face as he spoke. He came across as totally honest. To watch this big man, who I'd seen lift impressive amounts of weight at the gym, talk to me about being humiliated by the cops, struck a sympathetic chord in me. I was also impressed that, after getting out of jail, he had taken the initiative to look for witnesses. And on a personal level, what made me eventually decide to take the case, was Doug's story of the date—completely ruined—with the model, a woman who would never give him a second chance. There was something poignant about it. All of this pain and suffering for what? He didn't even get the girl!

In the end, Doug Stevens's case came to trial, and he was awarded $10,000. Why such a blatantly paltry amount? He should have received a larger settlement for such an egregious violation of his civil rights. But, it's consistent with what I've seen over the years. A black person with no money, no skills, will never receive very much money from a jury, because to them it's like giving him too much. They might think they're being generous, giving this poor black man a lot of money—$10,000. What's $10,000 going to change for Stevens? He's still a young black man living in Oakland. The case itself was tried in San Francisco, across the Bay. Although quite close to Oakland in proximity, San Francisco doesn't have the same issues, the same perception of the police department that the vast majority of people have in Oakland.

This was before the Rodney King case received national attention. Prior to Rodney King, most of these incidents got no press, as it was usually just one man's word against the whole department.

When I stood before the jury, I asked them to really look at Doug Stevens, the person. The man who suffered, the man who didn't get the girl. That was something tangible that I could use to show how a man's life, his hopes, could be destroyed by a police officer blind to everything but the color of his skin.

Doug Stevens had plans for that evening. He was optimistic. After all, how often do you get a date with a model? It sounds almost corny, but it really was a big deal to him. And, through no fault of his own, that date, that opportunity, that feeling of optimism, was taken from him. What's $10,000 going to change about that?

Keep On Keepin' On

In preparing his story for this book, I asked Doug Stevens to meet me at the scene of the incident. He has long since moved to another neighborhood, and it had been years since the last time he'd been there. Getting out of his car, the expression on his face was somber. "Man," he said, "this brings back a lot of memories, just being here."

Buried emotions and deliberately repressed memories quickly return, even after many years. Doug was able to recall with perfect clarity what took place years back. When his case went to court, the story was repeated over and over again. Every detail was examined under a microscope. All of this helps to seal the memory of these traumatic events in the minds of those who suffered them. It's one of the toughest prices exacted by the process of justice.

Doug, standing on the very spot where he had stood years earlier, began talking about what had happened that evening. His words sounded forced, as if he were reading his own deposition years later. It was difficult for him to distance himself from the past, and talk about what he was feeling *now*. A part of him was still having a hard time coming to terms with what had happened.

"I still feel raw. I was vulnerable. I couldn't do anything. They won. They did what they wanted to do to me. You know what I mean? I felt that another human being did something to me and they weren't reprimanded. They got away with it. They did it, and they're free to do it again."

It was one of those scorching late-summer days, so hot that

there was nobody around but the two of us. There was little to evoke the atmosphere of that evening years ago. In the end we only spent a few minutes there before moving on, finally giving in to the intense heat. But returning to that spot made me realize that the victims of these beatings never really get a sense of closure. To go to court is a positive experience for the victim, empowering up to a point. But in most cases the victim can see that justice isn't really served. The police officers involved usually get by without any serious reprimand. And, of course, nobody ever apologizes. As a result, a perfectly good guy like Doug Stevens, who was never going to be a problem for the police, can never feel comfortable around them again.

Now, inspired by the court process, Stevens is more involved than ever in the community. He speaks to groups of kids about his experiences. He talks to young men who have had trouble with the law. He explains to them what he went through, what he saw in court, and what he learned from the process. He is one of those who refuse to let such an incident become a dark stain on their lives.

"What doesn't kill you only makes you stronger, you know?" reflects Stevens. "And the whole process, I guess it was a message. It was sent from God. It was something that opened my eyes."

When I ask Stevens what has motivated him to get involved, he replies, "Somebody has to be concerned, and I'm just a concerned person. Especially because I went through it. I know firsthand."

BEING THERE

In the lingo of the streets, it's called DWB—Driving While Black—or WWB—Walking While Black. This refers to what many blacks believe to be the true nature of the charges made against them. They fit the "profile," they fit the stereotype. It happens every day.

Walking while black also has a number of attendant dangers. Walking in the "wrong" neighborhood at the "wrong" time of day is a definite police attractant. In some neighborhoods, any blacks who are not obviously female domestic workers are viewed with above-average suspicion. A perfect example is a case I had a number of years ago. A forty-two-year-old black man was walking home from a friend's house in San Rafael. As he was walking, he passed a young white woman who was in obvious distress over her car. She was fiddling with the key in the door, but couldn't get it open.

It was a sunny Saturday afternoon, broad daylight, and he was a nice man. He stopped. "Miss, excuse me. But could I help you? You look like you could use a hand." She didn't shoo him away or say no thanks. Instead, she said, "I can't seem to get it open." So he started fiddling with the key.

A police patrol car happened along, and the officers decided that the scene looked suspicious. That might have been reasonable, but the officers didn't stop to find out what was really going on. Instead they raced up, jumped out of the car, and one of the officers yelled at my client, "Step away from the car. Keep your hands where I can see them. Now, step toward me. Come over here."

My client was flabbergasted, especially when he noticed that the second officer was in a defensive crouch next to his car, with his hand on the butt end of his holstered pistol. As he walked toward the officer, hands up, my client said, "Excuse me, Officer. What's the problem? I was just trying to help here. I don't even know this lady."

Suddenly, the cop crouched by the car yelled, "Freeze. Stay right where you are!" And then the two cops rushed him, wrestled him to the ground, beat him, and took him to jail. He was charged with resisting arrest, soliciting prostitution, a whole slew of charges that were dismissed without comment a day or two later. The actual charge? Walking while black, in the wrong neighborhood.

The same is true of DWB—Driving While Black.

One of the most famous recent DWB cases involves Jonny Gammage, the first cousin of professional football player Ray Seals of the Pittsburgh Steelers. Pulled over by the police while driving Seals's late-model Jaguar, Jonny Gammage was beaten and suffocated to death by five Pittsburgh-area police officers. He was dead seven minutes after they'd pulled him over. His crime? Apparently Jonny Gammage committed no crime— except driving a late-model Jaguar while black.

The result? A series of sensational trials and acquittals for the officers involved, and a series of shocking revelations following the trials that suggested collusion between the forces of law and order. The entire Pittsburgh incident offered a revealing glimpse into the way the police, the district attorney, and the courts themselves, can manipulate the system to suit their purposes. The court and district attorneys often serve as de facto supporters of the police point of view.

The symbiotic relationship that exists between the police and the district attorney's office needs to be looked at in a new and harsher light. Of course local prosecutors are apt to give the police the benefit of the doubt, even in the most egregious examples of misuse of force: shootings, beatings, or murders.

To some extent it's understandable—the standard to prosecute a criminal case is substantially different from that of a civil case. And the DA's office is reluctant to prosecute police officers. When I handled the Rodney King case, it was clear that the local prosecutors didn't want to go through with it. There was clear and overwhelming evidence, and they didn't want the case. They didn't have the desire to see it through, and I think it's because police and prosecutors work so closely together.

The district attorney's office can't function effectively without a smooth and contiguous relationship with the police. The officers assist the DA by doing the legwork and compiling evidence and documentation that enables him or her to bring indictments. The police assist the DA throughout the entire process. Maybe it's asking too much of the DA's office to critically evaluate police conduct.

The general public doesn't always seem to fully comprehend this intimate relationship, so when the DA comes back with a vindication of an officer's questioned conduct, it's viewed as a complete exoneration, when in truth there may be clear violations of policy and procedure. Such violations, serious as they may be, do not necessarily rise to the level of criminal conduct necessary for the DA to bring charges.

Across the country, WWB and DWB cases are common-place. Occasionally, they flash across our TV screens, creating a brief wave of public uproar and indignation.

- Four young black men are driving down the New Jersey Turnpike on their way to a basketball tryout. Their van is peppered with a hail of police gunfire—before a word is spoken, or an order given. The van is later found to contain basketball equipment and a Bible.
- In Knoxville, Tennessee, thirty-four-year-old Andre Stenson, who has a heart condition, ends up dead after being stopped for a minor traffic violation.
- In Detroit, Malice Green is pulled from his car and beaten to death by two white police officers. The officers are con-victed, but in a second trial both are exonerated.
- College student Larnell Bulls is stopped while walking down the street in Pittsburgh, and held at gunpoint while he is roughly (and illegally) searched.
- Also in Pittsburgh, Tracy Liller, a disabled mother of six, is stopped on a traffic violation, handcuffed, and partially strip-searched in front of many male officers.
- In Philadelphia, Charles Thompson is stopped for running a stop sign, then severely beaten with blackjacks—after he is thrown on the ground and handcuffed.

You Run, You Pay

There's a variation on the theme of walking and driving. It's running. Every young black man knows this absolute fact: You run, you pay. It doesn't matter if you've done nothing. When a cop approaches you and you run away, he's going to go after you. And at the end of your run there will almost always be a beating, maybe an arrest, maybe worse. The very officers who will beat the hell out of a man like Doug Stevens, who was just walking down the street, don't understand that the result of that brutality might lead other black men to run away—not because they're guilty of a crime, but because they're scared of what might happen to them for just being there.

Everyone knows why Rodney King got beaten with such ferocity. He ran. He caused the adrenaline of the chase to course through the veins of his pursuers. It was his "fault," and he paid the price.

The chase is not without historical precedent. We can still close our eyes and call up the memory of black men running from packs of barking dogs along rural roads; running from men with guns, in hot pursuit. There is an added quality of humiliation involved in running when you know your last breath is held in the sights of a rifle.

On June 29, 1995, Bobby Fortune was walking down a street in Detroit when a police vehicle pulled up alongside him. Two officers emerged and began to question him in a harassing manner. Finally one of the officers, gloating at the frightened young man, said, "You look like you want to run. Go ahead, run."

Fortune ran, and the officers chased him down. They beat, kicked, and stomped him—broke his ribs, fractured his nose, and cut up his face. Later they filed charges against him for resisting arrest and obstructing a police officer. The charges were ultimately dropped.

One of the saddest cases I've ever dealt with that involved "running" was that of a nineteen-year-old kid named Baraka Hull. Baraka's run ended in death, the back of his neck pierced with a cop's bullet. For the rest of her life, Baraka's mother, Brenda Curry, will continue to nurse a sorrowful regret—if only her child had not run.

A shrine marks the spot where Baraka Hull was cut down by a policeman's bullet as he ran through a tattered patch of lawn across the street from his home.

Brenda Curry: "In Swahili, *Baraka* means 'blessing and prosperity.' He was truly a blessing to me."

I visit with Brenda on July 30, 1998, the fifth anniversary of her son's death. We stand together on the hot sidewalk, next to the little shrine so lovingly crafted and maintained by Baraka's friends. On the sidewalk beneath the shrine, someone has carved a heart and the words, *Baraka, we love you.*

"He was nineteen," Brenda Curry remembers. "A mother doesn't expect to bury her only child. It's supposed to be the other way around. And I had a lot of hopes and dreams for my son. He was going to school and he was working—and he was beginning to understand what it meant to be a man, and the importance of self, and trying to make it, and trying to be a good citizen. He didn't deserve what happened to him. My son was shot in the back. They don't shoot dogs in the back. They shot my son in the back for one reason—because he ran."

Baraka's unnecessary death capped an otherwise uneventful summer day. He and a buddy were sitting in a car and talking a few hundred feet from Baraka's house. Both had had minor skirmishes with the law in the past, but now they were employed, and Baraka was going to school. Becoming a father had softened his early rebellious streak and he was looking at the future with more mature eyes. Still, he had his moments of youthful foolishness, and this was one of them. Several months earlier, Baraka and his friend had procured guns for protection. The neighborhood they lived in was burdened with the specter of crime. Drug traffickers openly flaunted their wares. But Baraka's little corner of the world, shabby though it may be, was home. The neighbors looked out for one another. It was a community.

Suddenly a police car cruised by the boys and stopped. As an officer began to get out of his car, Baraka remembered the guns in the glove compartment. They'd be in big trouble if the cop found them. Baraka made a snap judgment to put some distance between the cop and the gun. Tucking the guns inside his pants, he jumped out of the car and sprinted across the tiny yard on the corner.

Officer Gildo Tournour, one year on the job, made a snap judgment, too—that Baraka was armed and dangerous, and probably a drug dealer.

Later Tournour would say that, in a move reminiscent of

the case of Melvin Black, Baraka turned while he was running, and pointed, as if to fire a gun. The many eyewitnesses tell a different story. Tournour crouched behind a tree, pointed, and fired straight through the back of Baraka's neck.

Ignoring the many eyewitness reports of neighbors, the department and the DA's office concluded the shooting was justified. Brenda Curry wasn't willing to stop there. She wanted her day in court, and I took on the case.

THE TEARS OF A MOTHER

This case presented a challenge, and demonstrated the complexity of the issue of police shootings. It was clear to me that Baraka had made a mistake. He ran. But the officer made a mistake, too. I had to look at it from the officer's point of view: What did Baraka do to cause him to believe his life was in danger? One witness stated that she saw Baraka turn slightly and glance back at Officer Tournour. Perhaps in that instant Tournour spotted a gun and believed Baraka was a threat.

As I looked into the case I discovered some unsavory truths about Officer Tournour. In one incident, a white bystander came forward to report he had observed Tournour chasing a black youth and shouting, "Nigger, don't run!" When he caught up to the boy, Tournour pressed a gun to his head and said, "I could have killed you."

It seemed to me that Tournour, a relatively new cop, was entering police work with the gung ho attitude of a soldier in enemy territory. This was exactly the type of attitude that fueled the flames of police–community conflict. At the same time I couldn't accept that Tournour had assassinated Baraka in cold blood. He had believed his action was justified, and no matter how wrongheaded he might have been, I knew that a jury would give him the benefit of the doubt.

As I worked the case I kept crashing into the reality of the two guns that Baraka had in his possession. I couldn't make those guns go away, and I imagined how big and threatening they would look on display in a courtroom.

There were no good guys, no winners. A mother lost her son. A child lost her father. A kid who might have made it took a stupid turn. A cop made a snap judgment that ended in tragedy. Would anyone care about Baraka's life? I wondered. Would a jury?

With all the ambiguities of the case, the city attorneys were worried about it going to trial. Tournour was a wild card. They didn't know how his past racist conduct would sit with a jury. So we had a settlement conference, and the city made a substantial offer. The money would go to Baraka's child, Kenyatta, and maybe it would help her escape the fate of her father.

Today, Brenda is heartbroken and she is angry. There is no consolation for a mother who has lost her son. But her activist resolve is deepened, and there is truth in her words: "The police need to have understanding of the people that they're dealing with in the community," she tells me. "Not just come here and come to work and arrest and beat and shoot and maim. Be concerned. In order to be concerned, you have to live within this area and understand. They don't. They have a whole other perspective. As far as they're concerned, this is the jungle, they've come to the jungle. And what do you do in the jungle? You hunt and you shoot.

"So," she says, staring sadly at the sun-scorched patch of earth that is now a memorial to Baraka, "now that I have given my son up, the struggle is not over, as far as I'm concerned. The struggle is alive and well. And I'm here. And until I have no breath left in my body, I'll always continue to fight for equal rights, for human rights, for human dignity, for people to be treated like they're human beings."

THE TRIGGER

Most police officers never fire their weapons, but on the occasions when they do the impact on the community is immediate and shattering. On the continuum of force, there is nothing so grave and potentially polarizing as a police shooting.

I have been involved in many such cases, typically involving white police officers and black male citizens. I know two things for certain: one, police shootings are *always* complex; and two, most people just don't want to acknowledge the complexity. In the aftermath of a police shooting, there is outrage in the community, and defensive control in the police department, and each side locks into its own rigid position. Most people choose sides without knowing any details. This polarization makes it virtually impossible to find out the truth or to resolve genuine issues of police procedure and conduct.

In February 1999, four New York City police officers fired forty-one shots at twenty-two-year-old Amadou Diallo, while he stood unarmed in the vestibule of his building. The plainclothes officers, members of the Street Crime Unit, were acting on information that a serial rapist might be in the area. How they came to fire their weapons at Diallo, a hardworking African immigrant with no criminal record, is still a matter of speculation as of this writing. However, the ensuing reaction of the community and the city officials was painfully typical.

From the outset there was a roar in the community that this was a racist shooting by racist cops. Once that tone was established, there was no room for a reasoned discussion about how this tragedy occurred and how similar tragedies might be avoided in the future. The complexity of these issues was lost in the shouting match between police spokespeople and black community leaders.

I think it is damaging to the ultimate resolution of these conflicts when the black community accuses police officers of being racist when there is no clear evidence, apart from the race of the victim and the race of the shooter, to support the charge. Maybe the real issue is training, or the safety of automatic weapons, or the procedures used by the Street Crime Unit, but these issues have little chance of being aired in a highly charged racial environment. Meanwhile, the police department often exacerbates the situation by its refusal to acknowledge that mistakes were made and its knee-jerk defense of the officers before any facts are known. In police rhetoric, there is no room for admitting error, even though errors occur. What we're left with is one side calling the shooting an assassination and the other side calling it a justifiable use of force, and *neither* side is right.

The price exacted for walking while black, for driving while black, is heavy for some; others have developed a cool resignation. "You expect it, that's all," a young man told me recently. A successful businessman with a nice car, he shrugged. "If I'm going to drive this car, I know I'll be stopped every day."

This seems to be a hopelessly intractable situation. But even if a police officer has reason to stop a black person walking down the street, or pull over his or her vehicle, there is a code of conduct that must be enforced. Too many of these situations escalate to violent confrontations within brief moments of their beginning. Are the police looking for pitched battles to engage in with black citizens? It's as though too many officers haven't been trained in the policies and procedures of their departments.

Chapter 7

THE CONTINUUM

> *Violence is not power, but the absence of power.*
>
> —RALPH WALDO EMERSON

Some of the problems that exist between police and communities might be solved by changes in policy. However, most of the conflicts take place in situations where police officers are ignoring well-established policy and training. Most of my clients are the victims of excessive force in situations where little or no force was required. The officers did not follow the continuum-of-force regulations—an official police policy that establishes the degree of force with which a police officer is supposed to respond in any given situation.

The continuum-of-force policy dictates that the response of the police officer is to be *one step above* the degree of resistance or force the officer is being offered, or is in danger of meeting, from a potential perpetrator. In the police academy, it is one of the primary lessons in being a good police officer.

As I said, continuum of force is a big issue in almost every case I handle. I fight this out in court again and again, because the official version (from the police) is always going to show a clear and compelling reason for each degree of force used by an officer in a particular situation. Sometimes that means outright lying—such as when the police said Doug Stevens was drunk in order to justify their actions.

Frequently I discover that the use of force was offensive, meaning that there was no reason to escalate the situation and attack. Cases such as those of Robert Davis, Darrell Hampton, and Doug Stevens show a terrible misuse of power, and are totally outside the parameters of both the training officers receive and the official departmental policy on the continuum of force. But it happens all the time.

Police officers, as trained professionals, are supposed to assess the given situation and respond defensively. None of the degrees on the continuum-of-force table is supposed to be instituted as an offensive tactic or weapon. Here is a typical continuum-of-force table, in order of increasing intensity of response:

- *Verbal commands.* This is the first degree of the continuum of force—the officer orders someone to respond to his or her directions: "Raise your hands." "Freeze." "Get out of the car."
- *Hand control.* This involves a number of different kinds of holds to take physical control of a person. It is sometimes

referred to as hold command. People are grabbed, arms are twisted, wrists are twisted back—there are a number of different holds police use to try and gain control, usually leading to the handcuffing of a subject. Hand control is not necessary if the verbal command is responded to—unless there is a legitimate suspicion that the person in custody needs to be disarmed.

- *Chemical control.* Pepper spray and Mace are used to disable anyone continuing to resist arrest. Chemicals have always been controversial because, to guarantee safety, they require police officers to make evaluations on a par with medical specialists: Is the person on drugs or drunk? Does he or she have a heart problem, asthma, or another medical condition? Might a woman be pregnant? Chemical sprays can also be dangerously nonspecific. I've represented many people, including small children, who were the collateral recipients of pepper spray.

In the early evening of April 30, 1994, Charlie Yoakum, 30, was driving home from his girlfriend's house following a bitter argument. His twin three-year-old sons were in the car. He wasn't aware that his girlfriend had flagged down a police car and complained that he'd threatened her, but as he approached the home of his grandmother, Hattie Stillwell, a police car pulled up behind him. Two officers jumped from the car and one ran up to the driver's-side door with his gun drawn, shouting, "Put your hands up and get out of the car." He then pressed his gun into Charlie's face, directly under his left eye. Charlie's mother, Betty Thomas, who lived two doors down, saw the scene from a window and came running out.

Within seconds, the situation had escalated to a highly volatile scene. Charlie was frozen with fear, his hands on the wheel, afraid to move. Betty was screaming at the officers to let the children out of the car. The officer was yelling, "Get out of the car," while pressing the gun against Charlie's head. Charlie's aunt, Otis Stillwell, ran out to the street. Other family members and neighbors began to gather. Later, several of them would say that they feared the officer would kill Charlie if he made a wrong move.

Then the officer started spraying Charlie in the face with pepper spray, also hitting the children in the backseat. When relatives moved forward to protest, they were also sprayed. Willard Stillwell, Charlie's uncle, arrived at that moment (ironically, from a police athletic league meeting) and tried to calm down the officer. He was sprayed too.

Fortunately, the situation did not get any worse. The officer backed off, Charlie exited the car, and the children were taken to safety. The incident didn't lead to an arrest; Charlie simply walked away.

The family was outraged by the entire incident, but especially the indiscriminate use of pepper spray around young children. The Police Review Commission Board of Inquiry later determined that pepper spray was used in a punitive, retaliatory manner and was also indiscriminate. The regulations were clear on the point that pepper spray should only be used to protect an officer or another person from physical harm, or to bring an unlawful situation under control. However, the Stillwells were sprayed because they questioned the officer and expressed concern about the safety of Charlie and the children. Willard Stillwell would later say, "It was the officer who was out of control, not the crowd."

Last year the San Francisco Police Commission engaged in a heated debate over the use of pepper spray, and narrowly overruled a recommendation that it be banned. Police officials stated that pepper spray, when used properly, was a far more benign defensive weapon than a baton, and certainly less deadly than a gun. However, several council members and many residents pointed out that very often pepper spray is not used according to policy—in particular, spraying too much, too close to the face (the rule is at least three feet), and spraying in areas where small children are affected. Police officers are also required to wash out the eyes of those who are pepper-sprayed. (As you'll see in the following chapter, that is impossible to do in crowd situations.)

More serious problems can arise when pepper spray and Mace are used on belligerent drunks, drugged-out people on meth, crack, or PCP, and the violent emotionally and mentally disturbed. I'm currently involved with a case in San Francisco where the problems of indiscriminate pepper spray use are illuminated. There had been a burglary, the police came to investigate, and in the course of their investigation were led to Aaron Williams, who was high on drugs and irrational. He resisted the officers and put up a fight. The police pepper-sprayed him repeatedly before they were able to cuff him. Then they dragged Aaron out and put him facedown in the back of a police car. They were either poorly trained or didn't care that the facedown position can be deadly for a person who might have trouble breathing. He died in the car.

- *Stun guns.* Some departmental policies place the application of a stun gun before the use of chemical control on the department's continuum-of-force table. Like the chemical sprays, the effect of the stun gun is usually very dramatic. It reduces resistance completely and almost instantaneously. The use of a powerful electrical jolt renders most people helpless.

  It seems obvious—although it didn't occur to the police officers who stunned Robert Davis into submission before they had uttered a word, issued a command, or executed a hold—that stun guns should be used only when there is a need to subdue. And careful training is required. If you press a stun gun against a person's body, and deliver continuous jolts of electricity, the person can suffer severe burns.

  There's another point to be made about the use of a Taser. We had expert testimony in the Rodney King case that the electrical volts from the Taser contributed to the involuntary movements that police officers interpreted as non-compliance. It was a real catch-22 for King.

- *Batons and flashlights.* The baton is the most dangerous of the impact weapons wielded by the police; the long, heavy-duty flashlights many officers carry are a close second. The officers are trained to use these weapons on the arms, thighs, legs, and the joint areas of subjects resisting arrest. Struck by weapons such as these on any of those areas, the subjects will experience crippling, disabling pain. Police are specifically told not to use these weapons on the head, face, or neck area, because of the potential for serious injury, but those instructions often are ignored. Cops will justify their actions by claiming they were defensive in nature: "I had no choice. He lunged at me just as I was swinging my baton at his elbow, and his face took the full blow. I went to strike him again on his arm, and again he moved, causing my baton to land squarely on the back of his head."

So many of the cases I've handled have involved head injuries. No matter what's said, there's usually no basis for striking someone on the head or face, except, of course, to inflict the most pain and to stop them cold. There's a clear policy that heads and faces are to be avoided. Officers are specifically trained to avoid the head, and yet it's usually the first place they hit.

Why? It's an automatic response. It's where they know they have the best opportunity to inflict damage, where they know they can most easily cause severe pain. A baton or a flashlight swung with power at someone's head will hurt them, and hurt them badly. It will bring a lot of people under instantaneous submission, sometimes toppling them to the ground. The aftermath of these kinds of blows is equally dramatic. People have subsequent concussion head-aches for months, sometimes years, sometimes forever.

• *The Chokehold, aka The Carotid Restraint Hold.* There's always been tremendous controversy about the use of chokeholds. There's no question that if a forearm is brought over the trachea and enough pressure is applied, the subject of the hold will die from asphyxiation. The carotid restraint hold is a supposedly safe variation of the chokehold, and is supposed to be a viselike grip of the inside joint of the arm across the subject's carotid arteries, which lie on either side of the neck, slightly forward of the ears. If the hold is applied correctly, it will render the subject unconscious due to lack of blood flow to the brain. It's a big "if," because if the hold is incorrectly applied, it will result in death.

If police officers are to continue using the carotid restraint—and I wonder why they must when pepper spray and stun guns are available—serious attention should be paid to training. It is an extremely precise maneuver, and the deaths mount every year from its use.

- *Deadly force.* The last resort on the continuum-of-force table is deadly force. Once an officer's weapon has been drawn from its holster, they are trained to shoot to kill, if necessary. It's surprising, really, how rarely officers ever fire their weapons. For that reason, most cases involving deadly force are deemed justified—even when a suspect was running away. Sadly, we've also learned that the notion of deadly force can spread to other points on the continuum. Virtually every use of force—except giving orders—can be deadly when it is not applied appropriately.

MARTIN'S LAST DAY

The Trahans were a struggling family, but a family nonetheless. Mary Trahan worked for the post office, and was the stabilizing force in the household. She and her husband, Martin, had been childhood sweethearts down in New Iberia, Louisiana, and had been married for twenty years, almost since they were kids.

They'd moved to Oakland, California, along with a large

group of Iberians, and settled in a neat, well-groomed neighborhood, with tidy lawns and painted fences. It was just the kind of working-class place where a respectable, struggling, lower-middle-class family could raise their children without fear. The neighbors were a close-knit, extended family. Everyone knew and watched out for one another. Kids ran back and forth among many welcoming houses.

Thirty-nine-year-old Martin Trahan worked a few different jobs. He was sometimes a janitor, occasionally a school aide, and frequently a storage mover. He tried to be a good father to his three children, reading to them and jogging around the block with them. He was also the family cook. His only problem was a fondness for cocaine that seemed to have gripped him suddenly in midlife. Martin developed a sizable habit, and his behavior became increasingly erratic and bizarre.

It had gotten bad enough a few times to make Mary decide to take out a temporary restraining order against Martin, which she only enforced when he was on a bender. Over the past few years, she'd also had to call the police three or four times, but only when Martin was completely wild.

Most of the time, though, Martin was fine. He was welcome at home and was an active part of his family. I wouldn't want to give the impression that he was a derelict. Far from it. In fact, only one of their three children, nineteen-year-old Elisa, was even aware of her father's problem. The other two children, twelve-year-old Khalylah, and especially six-year-old Martin Jr., were completely oblivious to their father's failings.

When he approached his home at around three P.M. on the afternoon of Monday, August 1, 1989, Martin Trahan had no idea what he was about to face. The facts are fairly straightforward. He was clearly under the influence of narcotics when he walked up to the door, calling out for his wife. Martin's younger daughter, Khalylah, told her father that her mother wasn't yet home from work. Martin started playing with Martin Jr., roughhousing, as they always did. Martin picked up his son and began swinging him around the front yard. This frightened Khalylah. She thought her father was acting crazy and wild, and might drop Martin Jr. Khalylah went into the house and told her older sister, Elisa, who was talking on the phone.

Asked later, Martin Jr. said that his father had just been playing with him, and he didn't understand what his sisters had been frightened about. He and his dad always played like that. But aware of her father's on-and-off use of cocaine, and the restraining order that was to be instated if he ever arrived home under the influence, Elisa got off the phone, looked out the window at her father and her brother in the front yard, and decided to call the police. She told the dispatcher who answered her call that her father needed help, and explained about the restraining order, and the way Martin was playing with his son.

After she got off the phone, Elisa followed the instructions she'd been given by the dispatcher. She got her sister Khalylah and went into the front yard, where she got Martin Jr. He and his dad were laughing and yelling when she came out at first, but Martin didn't give his daughter any trouble. Elisa took Martin Jr.'s hand, and the three children went next door to a neighbor's house. Martin had no idea what was going on, so he just went inside the house, got a cold drink, and sat down in the living room to wait for Mary. She was later than usual that day. It felt good to sit down and take a breather, though. Martin was soaked with sweat from playing with his boy.

Thirty minutes passed before a police car arrived. The police showed up just as Mary Trahan was returning home from work, unaware of the situation. By all accounts, Martin had calmed down by this point. When he saw the police car pull up, he was nonplussed. He walked out onto the front steps.

"What did I do? Why are the police here?" he asked his wife. Two black policemen, Abner Brewer and Willie Mc-Dowell, came up to Martin and directed him to go and sit in their cruiser. Reluctantly, Martin obeyed their orders, although he objected to getting all the way inside the police car. The children came over from next door, and Mary took them into the house.

Not long after they'd gone inside, a neighbor, V. J. Davis, came rushing into the Trahan house. "Mary, you got to come outside—the police are killing Martin!" V.J. screamed. "They're killing him!"

Somehow, Martin Trahan had found himself at the center of a tremendous battle with police officers on the street in front of his middle-class home, with the entire neighborhood looking on. The confrontation that day ended up involving a dozen police officers at one point, with police helicopters swooping down and surveilling from overhead. It's hard to believe that one barefoot, weaponless man, walking peacefully out of his house, could be the focal point of such a whirlwind of police activity. Martin Trahan's offense that day simply boiled down to coming home high on cocaine, and then spinning his son around in his front yard.

There are differing versions of exactly what happened, but among the disparities there remains one piece of irrefutable evidence: Martin Trahan, by the end of that day, lay on a slab in a refrigerated room of the local morgue. He had been choked to death—asphyxiation due to blunt trauma and compression of the neck, the result of a police officer's untrained or unforgiving use of the carotid hold.

Here is what happened. After being called to the home of the Trahans, Oakland police officers Abner Brewer, Willie McDowell, William Wallace, and other Oakland police officers, assaulted and beat Martin Trahan. As he cried, "Help me, they're killing me," he had his hands outstretched on a police car, following their orders. Once he'd assumed the outstretched position, they beat at his hands, head, and body with their batons. Even after they'd handcuffed his hands behind his back, they continued to beat him. When Mary Trahan rushed forward, screaming and hysterical, and begged the officers to stop beating her husband, they told her to shut up. Then they put her in the back of a police cruiser and threatened to take her to jail.

While this was going on, one of the officers began inflicting the illegal chokehold on Martin Trahan that crushed his trachea. Then the police officers threw Martin facedown on the ground, hands still cuffed behind his back. Once he'd stopped writhing, they left him there for a good ten to fifteen minutes before checking on him. When they finally turned him over on his back, took off the cuffs, and attempted CPR, it was too late. The officer who eventually turned him over was reported to have exclaimed disgustedly, "Oh, shit!" Martin Trahan was dead.

This was clearly an incident in which police officers used unnecessary and excessive force. The legal rhetoric, as it's usually laid out in court documents, goes on to state that they "wrongfully, intentionally, maliciously, willfully, wantonly, oppressively and without any just cause, assaulted and battered Martin Trahan." In the Trahan incident, witness after witness swore to the fact that Martin didn't fight with the police. He never even raised his hands to hit them. Apparently, Martin Trahan was calm, fairly submissive, and, even while doing as they ordered, he continued asking the police what he had done wrong. In the scheme of things, this was a minor domestic dispute, which should have involved the enforcement of the temporary retraining order. Inexplicably, it instead escalated into a show of overwhelming—and deadly—force.

No matter what might have actually happened, there is a softened, sanitized tone to police-department descriptions of events that day. Officers describe trying to "coax" Martin into the police car, describe how they tried to "explain" to him about the temporary restraining order. According to Officer McDowell, he took out his long baton to use as a "come-alonger." In account after account by the police, the protracted death struggle of Martin Trahan is reduced to pat, bloodless phrases—"a prolonged struggle ensued"—and then, one reads chillingly, "Martin Trahan suddenly became quiet and not moving." Some of the actions of the police officers are omitted entirely, as if Martin had begun his dance of death alone, in a distant world. One police officer, who arrived at the scene later to assist, stated categorically that he did not observe any strikes or blows. Other officers claimed that Martin continued to resist arrest, even after he'd been handcuffed and lay beaten on his neighbor's front lawn.

The autopsy revealed, among other injuries, five areas of blunt trauma to the neck, two scalp contusions, the skull crushed and flattened, the brain smashed and swollen, and—typical of a choking death—there was petechial hemorrhaging (spots of blood bursts in the eyes), pulmonary edema (accumulation of fluids in the lungs), and extreme congestion (swelling of tissues in the lungs and trachea).

Along with clinical details of his death, the autopsy noted a tattoo. The name Mary Ellen, his wife, was inscribed on Martin Trahan's back, over the scapula area.

We were left with the questions: Where was the continuum of force in this confrontation with Martin Trahan? At what point did the officers decide they had to use force? Which officer used what kind of force? Why? When did the baton become more than a "come-along" prod? When did it become necessary to strike Martin Trahan? When did it become necessary to restrain Martin Trahan with an illegal chokehold? When did it become necessary to leave him facedown on the ground, hands cuffed behind his back, after he'd been beaten with batons and had a chokehold applied?

What might have been done instead? Trahan posed no immediate threat. Could the officers have talked him down from his agitated state—if he was indeed agitated? Could they have called medical personnel—paramedics—to the scene to handle Martin Trahan, rather than trying to handle him themselves? There is always room along the continuum.

The City of Oakland settled with the Trahans, but the tragedy of Martin Trahan's death is that it didn't have to happen.

This was a clear failure of training. Police officers are trained to be forceful and proactive, but sometimes a circumstance demands that they step back and wait, or use quiet persuasion.

Several years after Martin's death, I had a case that underscored the need for a multidimensional approach. Charles Vaughn was a sixty-year-old black man, a paranoid schizophrenic who lived alone in Seaside, California. He functioned moderately well as long as he took his medication, and a social worker was assigned to monitor him. On May 19, 1998, the social worker reported that Vaughn had stopped taking his medicine, and mental-health personnel requested police assistance in having him committed to a treatment facility. When the police arrived, Vaughn became quite distressed and he fled to the roof of his apartment building. Two police officers followed him, and one began spraying Mace into his face. Vaughn was terrified, and he repeatedly cried for the police to leave him alone, and began to talk gibberish. When one of the officers approached him with a gun drawn, Vaughn held up what appeared to be a corkscrew, and the officers opened fire. Vaughn was shot four times; he died instantly.

I thought this case was outrageous. Here was a mentally ill man—clearly delusional, and of no real danger to three fully armed police officers. Furthermore, their reason for being there was to save Vaughn's life, and instead they killed him.

I filed a civil suit on behalf of Charles Vaughn's family, after the officers were cleared of any wrongdoing by the department. If this incident was an example of following procedure, I wanted to challenge the procedure. I was disturbed that the officers themselves were the aggressors. They did not approach Vaughn at the outset with due consideration of his mental state. Once he was frightened and paranoid, they did not have to follow him to the roof. They could have requested assistance from mental-health workers, or backed off and waited until Vaughn was calmer. It was my hope that this case (which is still being litigated as of this writing) would force the department to institute serious training and policy guidelines for dealing with the mentally ill and emotionally disturbed.

The cases of Trahan and Vaughn represent a fundamental lack of regard for the most vulnerable and damaged among us. We give police officers authority to use as much force as necessary, even deadly force, but unless an officer is able to use *no* force when that is appropriate, he cannot responsibly be trusted to use *any* force.

Chapter 8

THE BLACK SEA

I am an invisible man. No, I am not a spook like those who haunted Edgar Allan Poe; nor am I one of your Hollywood movie ectoplasms. I am a man of substance, of flesh and bone, fiber and liquids—and I might even be said to possess a mind. I am invisible, understand, simply because people refuse to see me.
—RALPH ELLISON, *INVISIBLE MAN*

Lake Merritt is a tranquil stretch of blue that winds in a lazy oval around the heart of Oakland. For many years I have run on the paved track that covers its 3.2-mile circumference. Lakeside Park is a lush green haven abutting the south-

Anthony Knuckles; a quiet spot on Lake Merritt.

east side of the lake. It is a place where kids play ball, where workers from the nearby Alameda County Courthouse linger over lunch on summer days, where young couples stroll.

The Lake Merritt area is home to some of Oakland's prime real estate. Charming town houses, towering high-rises, and picturesque, pastel-colored apartment buildings look down from the surrounding hills in a style reminiscent of Oakland's southern sister, San Francisco. Exclusive men's clubs, with their shiny brass door knockers and curtained bay windows, sit across from the park.

Every year, at the beginning of summer, Lake Merritt is the centerpiece of a citywide celebration. The Festival of the Lake has become a regular three-day event that draws about 100,000 people from all over northern California. The park is alive with the beat of music, the sizzle of food on the grill, and the mingled laughter and screeches coming from rides and games. It's a family affair, for young and old alike, but especially for the young.

Sunday, June 5, 1994

It was a beautiful day in Oakland, warm and balmy, with a cooling breeze blowing east off the Bay. The mood at the festival was giddy with the anticipation of summer—kids out of school, young men and women home from college reunited with old friends.

If the police presence was especially heavy that year, people tried not to let it dampen the mood. But you couldn't miss the faint undercurrent of tension. Kedar Ellis, a college student who worked as a security guard at the festival on Saturday, had noticed it. Since his family lived in the neighborhood, he knew what it was about. During the past few months, the police had been cracking down on young black people who came to the lake. The upscale residents had complained to the department that they didn't like so many black youths parking on their streets and walking through the area, goofing around and making noise. Recently the police had put a policy into effect, that outsiders couldn't park around the lake. They had also increased their presence in the area, essentially acting as street sweepers when they came upon black youths: "Move along. . . . Can't stop. . . . Move along."

Kedar Ellis had experienced this himself when he had been out walking with friends. There hadn't been any trouble yet, but the resentment was building beneath the surface. Kedar was considering going to law school, and he was sensitive to the questions of civil rights.

Even though the police were out in force for the festival, the first two days passed peacefully. Nearing the end of the final day, crowds of people were starting to leave the park when a fight broke out between two men. Several police officers rushed to break up the fight, and in the process of arresting one of them, beat him badly in front of a group of onlookers. People started to shout at the officers to stop hitting the man, who was already down, curled on the street like a rag doll.

At that moment, a car backfired. The cops claimed it was a gunshot, and suddenly the beautiful day turned sour. Police bullhorns blared, "This is an unlawful assembly. . . . The park is closed." A phalanx of riot-geared police came marching down the street, as if they had been dressed and ready all along. Black people started getting hit and beaten for not moving fast enough; they were arrested for just being there. Whites were let through without incident. A number of people I ended up representing hadn't even been at the festival. They were coming out of their homes, out of local bars, they were walking down the street just minding their own business when they got swept up into this maelstrom of baton-wielding riot police in full storm-trooper mode.

It was bedlam. The force of law pressing against an enormous crowd created fear, panic, and anger. An occupying force crashing through the mellow day, cracking heads, arresting anyone who wasn't moving fast enough. An army of blue on a black sea. Over 100 people were arrested in a little over an hour.

I hadn't been at the lake that day, but I saw a video of the incident on the evening news. It looked like a riot—a police riot.

"Can they do that, Daddy?" My young daughter's eyes were wide.

Could they?

In theory, yes. I tried to understand the way events had unfolded. You had large crowds—reports said 50,000 people—most of them heading out of the park. The police believed they had heard gunfire, and declared an unlawful assembly over loudspeakers. I knew they had the right to do that. But it's a big area. Some people on the far side of the lake couldn't hear the announcement; people driving up from the east side of Lakeshore couldn't hear it, either. Nonetheless, before they know it, the police are coming at them, pushing them with batons, ordering them to move, striking anyone who hesitated or didn't walk fast enough, indiscriminately using pepper spray.

Given that the police had a right to act under a declaration of unlawful assembly, the question became the manner in which they acted. Was it legal? Even if it was legal, was it appropriate? Who were the supervisors? What was the policy? What really happened?

I would begin to find out in the following weeks, as people started trickling into my office—indignant, wounded, looking for justice.

"Tell It to the Judge"

I was impressed with Kedar Ellis the minute he walked into my office. A handsome young man with an athletic build, well-mannered and bright, he reminded me of myself at that age. When he spoke, his words were measured, calm. I was touched by his honest effort to hold anger and recrimination in check—to simply recall what happened.

Kedar was a football player at Menlo College, and had graduated from the Oakland public school system. He lived within walking distance of the lake, and had worked as a security guard at the festival on Saturday, the day before the incident.

Sunday, he was walking down the hill from his house to meet three friends, and reached the street at the very moment

Kedar Ellis: "Our people had come through harsher difficulties. We had to be strong."

a blue wall of police officers was moving toward him, the fading daylight bouncing off the heavy plastic facial shields of their riot gear. Orders from bullhorns rippled along the pavement. "Move away. Move away."

Kedar was engulfed in a confused crowd, moving along, murmuring, "What happened?" Then a scream, and Kedar turned to see police on motorcycles that seemed to be roaring directly toward the crowd. Pandemonium broke out. People were running, yelling, and Kedar ran, too. But suddenly he stopped. Why was he running? He'd done nothing wrong. A police officer cut off Kedar's thoughts with a baton crack to his temple. And they were on him. Kedar caught a glimpse of a swastika tattoo on a burly arm. Heavy boots connected with his kidneys, and at some point his bowels let loose.

The cops dragged Kedar into a police car, where he waited until the paddy wagon pulled up and he was thrown inside. The wagon was crammed with young men. Kedar told me, "Brothers had been pepper-sprayed, beaten up. One brother was crying. I was crying, too, but I tried to calm people down."

I gave him a curious smile. "You did? How's that?"

"Well," Kedar answered, suddenly shy, "I just tried to say,

you know, this was bad, but we had to look deeper. Our people had gone through harsher difficulties coming here on slave ships, and most of them didn't even make it. We had to be strong, because we're their descendants. And we *were* going to make it."

He recalled his words without a hint of pretension, as if it were the most obvious thing in the world for someone to make this remarkable speech in a crowded paddy wagon filled with young black men. I marveled that a man so young could have achieved such dignity.

"It was hot and crowded in that van," Kedar went on. "I felt bad, because I had urinated and defecated on myself. So I told the brothers, 'If you guys smell shit, it's me, and I apologize.'"

I felt the familiar stirring—this man had been wronged.

I looked Kedar in the eye. "That's a tough story. So, what do you want to do? Are you looking for financial compensation? Is it the principle that matters?" I always try to learn a person's primary motivations. Civil suits are not for the faint of heart.

Kedar had a ready answer. "When I was sitting in the police car, I complained to the officer that I hadn't done anything, and this shouldn't have happened to me. I told him that the other cops had called me a nigger. And this cop, he just laughed. He said, 'Tell it to the judge.' So, I thought, *Okay, I will*. That's why I'm here."

In the end, I would represent fifteen of them. They were as fine a group of men as you'd ever want to meet. One after the other walked into my office, and I could see it before a word was spoken—the decency, the intelligence. Any one of them could have been my son, my brother, me. Every story had poignancy, some would live in my memory for many years.

Marcus McDade, coming out of a bar where he had just watched a Rockets–Knicks playoff game—struck with a police baton because he was not walking fast enough; Anthony Knuckles, paralyzed on his left side due to a preexisting condition—pepper-sprayed because he didn't move fast enough. Diallobe Johnson—beaten and arrested when he asked police officers why they were falsely arresting a friend. Patrick Simon, a forty-year-old local businessman and former Marine—also beaten up and arrested, for asking officers why

College student, Diallobe Johnson, was beaten and arrested when he questioned the police.

they were beating a young girl. Scott Patterson, a young photographer with a bad back, taking pictures of what was going on—also badly beaten. . . .

Seven would settle; eight would go to court. When I switched on the news the night before the trial started, a reporter was describing the upcoming court date, as scenes of the L.A. riots flashed across the screen. My stomach clenched. I got it. Invisible men in a sea of black.

A QUESTION OF POLICY

In every police case, I have two objectives in court. The first is to seek justice for my clients and to right a wrong. The second is to force change in the police department—whether the issue is crowd control, dog-bite policy, use of deadly force, handcuffing procedures, and so on. If policies are bad, let's reevaluate them. If procedures aren't being followed, let's find out why and fix it. If training is inadequate, let's improve it. And so on. Civil-rights law allows me to accomplish something of lasting value to the community.

So, as my team—Steven Collier, Matthew Kumin, Ted Harris, and myself—prepared the case and examined the evidence in its totality, we had to determine if the department itself was at fault. Most cases involve one or two cops, but that certainly wasn't the case at Lake Merritt. This was a departmental action, with many complex issues involved.

- *What was the policy for crowd control?* Simply put, how did police officers control and disperse a large crowd, disseminated over a wide area? Were the officers following a clearly stated policy? Did they have crowd-control training? And if so, what kind of training was it? When were those policies implemented? And did they practice these tactics regularly as part of their ongoing training?

  I soon discovered that the techniques for crowd control hadn't been updated since 1968, and that the manual used the language of the sixties, words like "mobs." I then discovered that, although those techniques were in the training manual, they never had been practically applied. In other words, the police never actually trained in any of these methods.

At one point during the trial, the police department's expert on crowd control testified that the department had a very clear crowd-control policy, modeled on a new policy put forth by the Criminal Justice Commission. He insisted that Oakland was consistent with that policy. During the cross-examination, I was able to elicit from this expert that the new policy hadn't been put into effect until eight months *after* the incident at the festival.

This was an important point because, in the state system, the city is always automatically responsible under a theory called "respondeat a superior." "Respondeat a superior" works like this: The principal—the city—hires someone— an agent—to do something for them. In that case, whatever the agent does—the principal is responsible for that action. Under federal civil-rights law that's not the case. An officer is considered responsible for his actions as an officer—the city isn't responsible unless there was a policy in effect that caused the officer's action.

• *What was the departmental actual plan for the festival?* When I examined the plans the police had drawn up for that day, I found that other than a heavy police presence, no particular consideration had been given to the potential need for crowd control. A friend of mine, who was a police- practice expert and the former chief of a police department in the Pacific Northwest, described the police tactics that day as inexplicable and amateurish. They had set up no intelligence posts, nor did they arrange for scouts. They had not executed a tactical placement of troops, and had no contingency plans for paddy wagons, ambulances, paramedic stations, or processing of people who were sick or injured—much less 100 prisoners. It was an amazing show of incompetence and lack of professionalism.

If there was any policy in place, it came under the vague, umbrella phrase, "zero tolerance." Move people along. Tolerate no resistance. Arrest people for so much as spitting on the sidewalk or loitering.

• *What was the policy on the use of pepper spray?* Pepper spray was a relatively recent innovation at that time. What policies on its use had been issued? What guidelines? What training had the officers had in using it? Was there a policy in effect for taking care of people who'd been pepper-sprayed?

This is what I discovered. The officers had been issued the pepper spray with a minimal amount of training. The only care required to be given to those who were pepper-sprayed occurred if the victim of a spraying had been taken into custody. Those not arrested weren't treated; that is, the spray wasn't washed from their eyes. Another question rose about the indiscriminate use of this pepper spray. Should pepper spray be used as a crowd-control technique?

• *What was the policy on dealing with the disabled?* This issue came up because of what happened to one of my guys. I believed that officers had violated the Americans with Disabilities Act.

Anthony Knuckles lived right up the street from the park, with his girlfriend, and his mother lived next door. On the day of the incident, it was Anthony's thirty-first birthday. His mother and sister wanted him out of the house so they could get ready for the celebration, so Anthony and his first cousin, Chester Meadows, walked down to the park, Chester wheeling his bike alongside. This wasn't a simple task for Anthony, who suffers from a neurological condition called arterial venous malfunction. He is basically paralyzed on his left side and walks with a limp. It's a neurological condition.

When they reached the bottom of the hill, Anthony sat on his favorite bench overlooking the full span of the lake. Within minutes, the two men were in the center of a maelstrom. A motorcycle cop pulled up to the bench and said, "Get out of the park. Move!" Anthony told him that he was paralyzed, and he could not move very fast, so the officer said, "Okay, follow me." But as Anthony and Chester were following the motorcycle, another cop came up, yelled, "Hey, boy, you're not moving fast enough," and pepper-sprayed Anthony, sending him down on one knee.

There was more, but you get the picture. Anthony was an impressive man, with a friendly nature, who had clearly transcended his handicap. The jurors were obviously taken with him. And when we examined departmental policies, we discovered that there had been no training in dealing with the handicapped, and no attention paid to the ADA law.

• *What was the quality of the supervision?* It seemed obvious to me that a case could be made for negligent supervision. The commander at the scene was a black police officer, Captain Meyers, who was on a motorcycle. If the officers had been properly supervised, there wouldn't have been the indiscriminate use of batons and pepper spray. The police reaction that day was way out of proportion to the events, and Captain Meyers was responsible for not reining in his people and keeping control of the situation. He, of course, claimed otherwise.

On the whole, the jurors concurred with our view of events, although the awards were small—and in a couple of cases, nonexistent. The trial took an emotional toll on the eight plaintiffs, but in the end most of them were glad they went through it.

From the start, I told them, what's important is standing up for yourself and not letting the police get away with that kind of behavior. First, you demonstrate that you have rights and second, you demonstrate that you have the courage to stand up for those rights. I think that's a pretty big deal.

A GOOD SOLDIER

Four years after the incident, Patrick Simon cannot speak about what happened to him without spilling over in an emotional surge of anger and hurt. I can assure you that Patrick is not a man who cries easily. He was a Marine, and everyone knows that Marines don't easily cry.

On a warm August day in 1998, Patrick and I go for a stroll along the lake. The sun is beating down, but Patrick is dressed in a perfectly pressed double-breasted white suit. He is always impeccable in this way.

He warns me, "This brings up a lot of emotion for me and

Patrick Simon: "It's about democracy."

I'm still getting some help for it." But I am not prepared for the ferocity of Patrick Simon's anger, as the words spill out of him.

"I did twenty years in the military. I'm a highly decorated veteran. I have three or four meritorious service medals, two or three commendation medals. My greatest award was the medal of heroism I received from the San Francisco mayor, Art Agnos. I got it for rescuing a woman who was trapped in the Federal Building during the 1989 earthquake.

"So, helping human beings and being an ambassador, a soldier—that's who I am. I've always tried to represent the United States, and I believe in what this country stands for—freedom, democracy, the ideals and the values that we all have instilled in us from many hundreds of years."

Patrick's words resonate because they are obviously so true, so heartfelt. After he retired from the military, Patrick used his VA benefits to go to night school, and he had just started a fiber-optics consulting company. He was in his office when he heard the noise, and he went to see what the commotion was about. There was bedlam. His eyes lit on a police officer dragging a young black woman across the street by her braids—as she screamed, he slapped her.

Patrick marched up to the officer and stared at his chest.

When the cop asked him what he was doing, Patrick responded, "Officer, I just wanted to get your badge number because what I just saw you do I don't think was right."

The officer grabbed Patrick, dragged him across the street, slammed him against a police car, handcuffed him, and threw him in the backseat.

As we walk along, Patrick reaches into his pocket and pulls out a card. His voice is wavering with indignation. "I managed to go in my wallet and I pulled out my retired-military ID card. I showed him this card and I said, Does this not mean anything in America? I'm a retired U.S. serviceman after twenty years of service. This is about democracy. This is about freedom. Why are you doing this to me?"

Patrick's throat closes, he struggles to hold back tears, but his words come out as a sob. "The officer said, 'That doesn't mean shit to me. It means nothing.'"

Patrick starts crying, and I awkwardly put my arm around him. What can I say?

As I drive back to my office, I think about the wounds that never heal, the shame of being invisible. Patrick Simon's service to America, the greatest pride of his life, is tarnished. He will never again be able to look at his medals and commendations, without hearing the words, "That doesn't mean shit."

WHERE CITIZENS GATHER

Police and citizens can learn from their mistakes. In the years following the incident at Lake Merritt, the festivals had a very different spirit. The police were friendly, mingling on foot among the crowds. There were no motorcycles, no threat of confrontation. Everyone understood that less was more.

If police departments overreact in crowd scenes, destruction and violence can become a self-fulfilling prophecy. Let's be realistic. When several thousand people are gathered in a contained area, be it for entertainment or a political rally, it is very easy for one or two people to instigate bedlam by the simple act of throwing a bottle or breaking a window. If the police respond with a show of overwhelming force against the entire crowd, the result will be exactly what the police are there to prevent. In effect, the police start the riot. If, on the other hand, the police response to isolated incidents is measured, the conflict will be minimized.

It sometimes happens that fundamental civil rights—in particular, the right to assembly and the right to speech—are viewed as threats to civil order by nervous police departments, especially when the gatherings have political overtones. We saw this in New York City in September 1998 with the so-called Million Youth March. The march, which ended up drawing only about 6,000 people, was a classic example of police overreaction in advance. Like a red flag to a bull, the march's leader, Khalid Abdul Muhammad, engaged in inflammatory speech that drove Mayor Rudy Giuliani and Police Commissioner Howard Safir a little crazy with anticipation. Safir issued a clear warning that there would be zero tolerance, and backed up his announcement by sending battalions of police officers in riot gear to the scene, telling them to disperse the crowd on the dot of four P.M. There was a clear expectation that the crowd, inspired by the speech of Khalid Muhammad, would riot.

In fact, the gathering was peaceful. Even Khalid Muhammad's vitriolic speech failed to produce any action, until the police moved in to disperse the crowd with a completely unnecessary show of force and confrontation.

Fiery speech doesn't give police permission to respond in a fiery manner. Cooler heads should prevail, both on the street and at the top.

Chapter 9

AIN'T I A WOMAN?

That man over there says that women need to be helped into carriages, and lifted over ditches, and to have the best place everywhere. Nobody ever helps me into carriages, or over mud puddles, or gives me any best place! And ain't I a woman?
—SOJOURNER TRUTH

Along with most other people, I once believed that the problem of police brutality could be largely remedied if we brought more minority and women officers into the community. Minority officers would be more understanding of the community environment, the lingo, the customs. Women are known to be more effective communicators and better listeners. They would be unlikely to participate in the "macho" clashes that so often occur between white cops and black men.

What I have learned, however, is that while minority and female officers have made some positive difference, the problem is much larger than individuals. I didn't account for the *culture* of the police—the way attitudes and behaviors infiltrate the academy, the station house, and the street.

Some female officers try harder to prove their toughness. They don't want to stand outside the loop; they want their gender to disappear once they put on the uniform.

Nothing has solidified my belief that we must seek change in the culture of the police, not just in individuals, more than the following two incidents. Both involved female victims, and both involved abuse by a particularly aggressive female officer.

THE RESPECTABLE JAYWALKER

Marguerite Martin was a gifted and caring young woman—a social worker and a doctoral student on her way to becoming a psychologist. In her work with substance abusers, she was a highly regarded professional, known for her dedication and hard work. Educated, dignified, married to a college professor, Marguerite developed certain assumptions about what she might expect from the world. She understood that life was filled with matters of chance—accidents and illnesses—that there was no way to guard against. She also knew that there was a lot of unfairness directed against blacks, although she had never really experienced it herself. She felt protected by her status and stature. But during a visit to California to attend a friend's wedding, her sense of security was shattered.

One afternoon, Marguerite decided to go shopping on Lake Shore Avenue, an upscale area with many charming little stores. Listening to her Walkman, she wandered into a dress shop, bought something, then saw another dress shop across the street. Rather than walking all the way to the intersection to cross, Marguerite crossed in the middle of the block. When she came out of the second dress shop, she saw a health-food store she'd noticed earlier, so again she began to cross the street. This time, however, a motorist called out and warned her to be careful, explaining that she could get a ticket for jaywalking.

Marguerite smiled and shrugged. A jaywalking ticket seemed quaint to her. Nevertheless, she dutifully walked to the intersection, crossed the street, and went into the health-food store.

While Marguerite was talking to the owner of the store, a young female police officer, named Inga Winkle, entered the store and belligerently approached Marguerite.

"I want to see your ID," Winkle demanded.

Marguerite was bewildered. "What's the problem, Officer?" she asked. The officer told Marguerite she'd seen her jaywalk. Marguerite smiled. So that was it. "No, Officer, I crossed at the light," she said. The officer was adamant. "I saw you jaywalking. Now, show me some ID."

"Look, I know what this is about. I crossed in the middle of the street a while ago, but some guy driving by told me to be careful, and then I went and crossed at the light." Marguerite then handed Winkle her West Virginia driver's license as identification. As Winkle began to write Marguerite a ticket, Marguerite said, in a lighthearted way, "I didn't realize that jaywalking was considered such a serious crime in California."

Winkle stopped writing the ticket, and gave Marguerite a

hostile look. "They have stop signs in West Virginia, don't they? And crosswalks?" Then she finished writing the ticket, and shoved it at Marguerite. "Sign it."

Marguerite would later admit that she didn't know why she suddenly felt threatened or nervous about signing the ticket. She should have just done it, but this police officer seemed to have something against her personally. Besides, she had been raised in New York, where jaywalking and parking tickets didn't have to be signed. "I don't think I have to sign it," Marguerite said, taking her driver's license out of Winkle's hand.

Officer Winkle had not begun their encounter courteously. Now, whatever weak tendrils of patience that had clung to her, snapped free. She became enraged, bellowed, "Okay, that's it!" and reached out and grabbed Marguerite.

In most cases of police misconduct, there's a series of events that lead to a culminating moment of great volatility, a balance point where the episode could have been handled differently and gone another way. Then violence erupts. With Marguerite Martin, that moment occurred when Officer Inga Winkle decided to get physical with her. As soon as Marguerite expressed that flash of baffled indignation and disbelief that anyone might feel when they find themselves being harassed by a police officer, the encounter became violent. Once Officer Winkle grabbed Marguerite Martin, her actions veered in a predictable direction. Having zipped through the continuum-of-force table and gone from verbal command to physical force, Winkle had left herself with few options. Grabbing Marguerite by her jacket, Winkle pushed her toward the back of the store, then slammed her face-first into a large refrigerator unit.

When Marguerite cried out, "What are you doing to me?" Officer Winkle replied, "I'm taking you in. You don't yank your ID out of my hand and walk away." Winkle reached for Marguerite's sleeve, and Marguerite reflexively pulled away. Winkle then grabbed Marguerite's forearm and upper arm with both hands. Marguerite struggled, crying, "Let go of me. You're hurting me! I'll sign the ticket." As Marguerite continued to struggle in a reflexive panic, Winkle grabbed her by the neck, then threw her down so forcefully that Marguerite's head hit the floor—hard.

Now Marguerite Martin was hurt and frightened. She screamed for help, tried to get up, and had made it to her hands and knees before Officer Winkle came up on her side, grabbed her arm and pulled it behind her back, twisting it upwards in what the officer later described in court as a "pain compliance" measure. Officer Winkle then placed her knee in the small of Marguerite's back, put all of her weight into it, and forced her flat onto the floor. Then she handcuffed her.

When she had both of Marguerite's hands cuffed, Officer Winkle dragged her through the store and outside, where several other police cars had gathered. There, Marguerite Martin—doctoral student, social worker, wife—was frisked for weapons by a male police officer in the middle of the street. Within a few moments, she'd been transformed from a dignified citizen into a shackled prisoner with no rights.

Officer Winkle's behavior was clearly unwarranted. Whatever their personality problems, hang-ups, or prejudices, officers are neither trained nor encouraged to inflate a technical violation that requires no use of force, into a confrontational situation.

Forty-five minutes after her confrontation with Officer Winkle in the health-food store, Marguerite Martin was sitting handcuffed in the backseat of a parked police car, bruised and aching, still not knowing what was going to happen to her, or even able to figure out what she had done to justify such treatment. Outside the car, now parked in a gas-station lot, four or five police officers joked with Officer Winkle. Several of the officers walked over and peered in at Marguerite curiously, as though she were a circus act on display. Finally Officer Winkle walked over to the rear window of the police car.

"What's going to happen to me?" Marguerite asked her.

"You're going to jail," Officer Winkle informed her flatly, "for resisting arrest. It'll be ten thousand dollars' bail." Officer Winkle then cursed at Marguerite and walked away.

To add further injury to Marguerite, the district attorney's office and the police department formed a shield of protection around Officer Winkle, and in so doing, chose to make an example of Marguerite. When the DA's office announced that it would bring criminal charges against Marguerite, she was horrified. A weekend wedding had turned into a full-fledged nightmare. If you think it's impossible to face a criminal trial for such an incident, think again. If found guilty, Marguerite could have been sentenced to a year in jail. She would have been locked up thousands of miles from home, and her career as a social worker would have been destroyed. This was dead-serious business.

Marguerite wept as she told me her story. She couldn't *stop* weeping. There was no place in her arsenal of internal resources to accommodate what had happened to her. That a police officer, another woman, would grab dignified Marguerite Martin, with her charming smile and unassuming manner, and drag her around in public like a rag doll, was so injurious to her, so contradictory to anything she had ever expected to encounter, that there was no way to quantify her emotional distress.

From the start I focused on the question, *Did Officer Winkle follow procedures?* I concluded that she had not.

Marguerite Martin should have been informed that signing her ticket was not an admission of guilt, but only a promise to appear in court. Officer Winkle should also have told Marguerite what her options were if she didn't agree with the violation. Despite Winkle's behavior, it was not a technical violation for Marguerite to argue her ticket. She was entitled to be given a reasonable opportunity to understand what she was being charged with. If she still didn't want to sign the ticket, Officer Winkle was obligated under departmental guidelines to call in a supervisor to assist her, instead of using force.

During that time, I had a number of police-practice cases that stemmed from jaywalking incidents. It never failed to astonish me that a police officer could turn such a benign situation into a use of force that resulted in injury. Once again, in the Marguerite Martin case, I saw a complete lack of respect exhibited, and an egregious lack of ordinary common sense on the part of an officer.

Also, Officer Winkle should have informed Marguerite

why she was being arrested later in their encounter. Since Winkle was making an arrest for something other than the citation, she needed to explain to Marguerite why she was escalating the incident to an arrest.

Officer Winkle appeared in court dressed in a feminine way. When she spoke, her voice was soft and low. She did everything she could to create an image of a gentle soul who would never be capable of belligerent, much less abusive, behavior. I was a bit offended by the "new" Inga Winkle—a visual lie.

Winkle claimed that Marguerite had spouted profanity at her in the health-food store while she was giving her the ticket. She stated that she had told Marguerite Martin what her options were regarding the ticket, and had explained that if Marguerite didn't sign the ticket, she was going to jail. She stated that Marguerite had resisted arrest by pulling out of her grasp and swinging a closed fist at her. And finally she said that she had never grabbed Marguerite's neck as she threw her to the ground.

In court, these points were refuted not only by Marguerite herself, but also by Paul Hong, the health-food store owner and an eyewitness to the entire event. He had been three to five feet away from the action that day. A doctor's examination showed definite signs of a neck injury, and tenderness in the area consistent with a grab to the neck. We also brought in a character witness, a coworker of Marguerite's, who testified under oath that she had never heard Marguerite use profanity in all the years they had been acquainted.

However, our biggest break was provided by Officer Winkle's own past. Because Marguerite's case became a criminal matter, I was entitled to look into Winkle's background. I found an incident that I thought would set the record straight about Inga Winkle's style of policing. The incident involved an elderly woman, Katzuko Ziomek, who possessed barely a rudimentary grasp of English, and who'd had the misfortune of encountering Officer Winkle.

Mrs. Ziomek was as perfect a witness as you could want. When she walked haltingly up to the stand and took the oath, the jurors' faces melted. She had the face of a grandmother, the demeanor of an honest, law-abiding citizen. In broken English, she told her story to the rapt courtroom.

In September of 1989, an animal-control officer for the city of Oakland arrived at Mrs. Ziomek's residence and tried to give her a ticket, claiming that a complaint had been made concerning her daughter's dog. According to the citation, earlier that day when Mrs. Ziomek had been out shopping, the dog had somehow gotten out of the gated yard and was seen wandering on the street.

Mrs. Ziomek insisted that wasn't true. The dog was inside the closed gate when she returned, and there was no way he could have escaped. She refused to accept or sign the ticket, and the animal-control officer called the police.

Later that day, as Mrs. Ziomek was hanging laundry on a line in her backyard, two officers approached her. One of them was Inga Winkle. Without questioning her, the officers demanded that she sign the citation. She again refused, insisting that the dog had been on her property the entire time.

Officer Winkle said sharply, "You're going to jail." Then she approached the old woman from behind, twisted her arm painfully behind her back, and dragged her from the backyard to the street. By the time Mrs. Ziomek reached the street, her stretch pants and her underwear had been pulled off, and were bunched around her knees. She was left there, exposed, for all her neighbors to see.

The heartrending account of Katsuko Ziomek provided the final blow to Inga Winkle's credibility. Marguerite was acquitted. Later, we filed a civil suit against the city, and it was quickly settled. Marguerite informed me soberly that she would never step foot in California again. I said to myself, *If only it were as simple as that.*

THERE BUT FOR THE GRACE OF GOD . . .

The damage a single bad cop can inflict is awesome. That the career of such a cop can endure despite a repeated history

Joyce Sept; her return to the scene of her abuse was an act of courage.

of brutality, is a tremendous failure on the part of the department.

By April 19, 1991, Marguerite Martin and Katsuko Ziomek had already endured their humiliating confrontations with Officer Winkle. Nevertheless, she remained on the street as a traffic cop, her bullying methods left unrestrained.

Joyce Sept, a hardworking mother of three, and a food-service worker at Fairmont Hospital, was driving herself to work, dressed in her white uniform, when she was pulled over for speeding by two Oakland Police Department motorcycle officers. Unfortunately for Joyce Sept, one of the officers was Inga Winkle. Officer Winkle demanded to see Sept's license and registration.

After pouring everything out of her purse and glove compartment, Joyce located her registration, but was unable to find her driver's license. But she knew her license number by heart and provided it to Officer Winkle, along with seventeen current credit cards, her checkbook, and her union card. Winkle wasn't satisfied with all of this identification, and insisted that a photo ID was necessary.

Joyce found a hospital-employee newsletter in her car with a picture of her on the front page, and her name under it, identifying Joyce Sept as Fairmont Hospital's Employee of the Month. Still, this wasn't adequate for Officer Winkle. She opened Joyce's car door and ordered her out of her car. As she got out, Officer Winkle told her that she was going to be arrested.

Joyce began to cry. "Arrested for what?" she asked. Officer Winkle said it didn't matter, to just turn around and place her hands on top of the car's roof. Winkle pulled Joyce's arms behind her and handcuffed her. Then she began pulling her around by the cuffs. Joyce cried harder, and begged Winkle to let her go, but Winkle just yanked at her cuffs and said, "No matter what you say, you're gonna be arrested."

There was a troubling subtext—that the officer was intrinsically above the law, and Joyce Sept below it.

Joyce's handcuffs were so painfully tight that she implored

Winkle to loosen them; they were cutting into her flesh. After consulting with her male partner, Officer Winkle told Joyce she would make her more comfortable. She removed the cuff on the left wrist, but kept the cuff on her right wrist. Then she roughly handcuffed Joyce's right arm to the top of a chain-link fence surrounding a vacant lot.

Weeping and publicly humiliated as friends and neighbors walked by, Joyce spent nearly an hour chained to the fence by the side of the road. It was a deliberately hostile and cruel action on Winkle's part. There was no logical reason for Joyce to be detained in this way. She was not an intimidating presence, and she certainly posed no possible threat. Still, Officer Winkle insisted she remain chained until a patrol car arrived. Despite Joyce's pleas, Winkle also ordered her car impounded.

When a transportation car arrived nearly an hour later, the patrol officer asked Officer Winkle for Joyce's name. In spite of the voluminous identification Joyce had presented, Winkle informed the transportation officer that she was an unknown—a Jane Doe.

Joyce was then driven to another location, where she awaited the arrival of a paddy wagon. When the wagon arrived, Joyce finally received a small mercy, thanks to a cop who was doing his job properly. The officer refused to take her to the police station. It was clear to him that she had presented enough verifiable identification to be cited and released. She was driven to her impounded car by another officer, where it was released to her without payment. She had been stopped at approximately eleven A.M., and wasn't freed until three P.M. A four-hour traffic stop.

When I heard about what had happened to Joyce it didn't surprise me to learn it had been Winkle's call to chain a young woman in a white hospital uniform to a chain-link fence, as if she could be treated without human consideration. It made my blood boil.

I put together an exhibit showing all the pieces of ID this so-called Jane Doe had had in her possession that day— including her face smiling from the hospital newsletter under the headline *Employee of the Month*. It was almost comical. I know *I* don't carry that much identification. If anything, Joyce was *over*identified. The city lawyers were impressed, and the case was easily settled. but it was a sad victory in a way, because Joyce was permanently traumatized by the incident.

Seven years later, when I asked Joyce to return with me to the site, and talk about what happened, she started to shake. "Oh, I don't know if I can go back there," she said. "I'm too scared." She confessed that she is still beset with fears of being harassed by the police, especially when she's in her car. "It's okay when I'm walking or when I see them at the hospital," she said. "But if I see police when I'm driving, I'll do anything to avoid them. I'll get off the freeway, turn corners, pull over and park." Joyce told me that not long ago, she had been a passenger in a car that was stopped by a cop. She became hysterical and started sobbing. The officer was alarmed. Joyce's friend told him why she was so upset, and he let them go without a ticket.

Joyce was scared, but she was brave. She finally agreed to return with me to the site of her encounter with Officer Winkle. She felt it was her duty to let others know what had happened to her—to stand tall for the sake of her children. She was shaking as we reached the chain-link fence, as if she were facing her worst enemy. But she walked over to it, reached out and wrapped her hand around a link. Smiling shyly, Joyce said, "See? I can do it."

Chapter 10

A FAILURE TO COMMUNICATE

He that will not reason is a bigot; he that cannot reason is a fool; and he that dares not reason is a slave.

—WILLIAM DRUMMOND

There are some people who just aren't suited to be police officers, but more often when I see an overly aggressive police officer, I see the product of poor training. Inga Winkle was only a twenty-four-year-old rookie when she encountered Marguerite Martin. At that point in her career, she was most likely mimicking a style of policing that she had seen practiced by more experienced officers.

Communication—a police officer's most potent weapon— is not stressed enough in academy or in field training. It is not to a police officer's credit when he or she escalates a situation that could easily be *de*escalated. In Marguerite Martin's case, the whole scene might have played out differently if Winkle had shown a modicum of courtesy in the first place, which is a sign of respect fundamental to any effective communication. Let's examine how the outcome of a similar officer–citizen confrontation might have been different. Imagine this hypothetical scene:

A police officer approaches a woman on the street.

OFFICER: Excuse me, ma'am. I noticed you jaywalking. May I see some ID?

WOMAN: I crossed at the light.

OFFICER: Before that, you were jaywalking.

WOMAN: Oh, I know what this is about. I crossed in the middle of street a while ago, but some guy told me to be careful and then I went and crossed at the light.

She hands the officer her driver's license.

OFFICER: You live in West Virginia?

WOMAN: Yes, I'm here for the weekend. My friend is getting married.

OFFICER: I'm going to write you a ticket.

WOMAN: I didn't realize jaywalking was such a serious crime here in California.

OFFICER: It's a violation. The regulation is for your safety and the safety of others.

She hands the woman the ticket, and asks her to sign it.

WOMAN: I don't think I have to sign it.

OFFICER: It's required. It doesn't mean you are admitting to guilt; only that you promise to appear in court or—since you're from out of town—otherwise take care of the ticket. Your options are on the back.

The woman signs the ticket and the officer hands her a copy and her driver's license.

Even if the woman continued to refuse to sign, which is doubtful in light of the officer's polite but firm handling of the situation, the officer could have radioed for a supervisor, saying to the woman, "Let me get my supervisor over here to explain it to you."

Let's take it one step further and say that the woman was belligerent. That she swore at the officer and refused to accept the ticket. In other words, she displayed what we call "contempt of cop." Many officers become outraged when they perceive that a citizen is being disrespectful to them. However, under the law, you *can* be disrespectful to an officer. You can use profanity, or you can shout at him or her. I've asked many cops in court, "Is it illegal for a citizen to shout at a police officer and use profanity?" They all said no. In fact, they are taught in the academy that some people will use profanity and yell and scream at them. That is not a basis for an arrest in a legal sense. But what actually happens on the street is that "contempt of cop" can lead to escalation because the police officer becomes angry.

If the woman in this fictitious scenario had actually launched a verbal attack, the police officer, *if* she had been properly trained, would have let it roll off her. She wouldn't have felt any less in control. In fact, her strength in that moment would have been enhanced by her cool demeanor. She might have said any number of things: "If you refuse to sign the ticket, I will have to keep your driver's license and you will need to come down to the station." Or, "I know you're unhappy about this, but you can explain your side to the judge." Or, "I must insist that you sign, or you'll have to come with me." Or, "If you refuse to sign, you'll have to wait here until my supervisor arrives."

In other words, she would have let the woman know that this wasn't going to go away—and that all of the options would be more disruptive to the woman's life than signing the ticket.

There are times, of course, when verbal communication won't work. But unless a citizen is in the process of committing a crime, or is suspected of being a danger at that moment, a police officer should always start by talking—in a calm, professional, and, most of all, respectful way.

During the training process there has to be significant time given to understanding the community which you serve. Field training officers who will show new officers the ropes have to be assigned, to inculcate in them a certain code of conduct and behavior that will serve them well.

Cops must be trained to act rather than react, to set aside their emotions, to respect the rules of law. Some of that ability comes with time and maturity, but a lot of it comes from watching senior officers who do it well.

The field training officer (FTO) is the new officer's first contact. New officers are molded by the initial training received from the FTO officers. What's acceptable? What isn't acceptable? If a training officer gives the message that black people don't listen to reason and can't be talked to, that your only option is to control them physically through intimidation or physical force, then that's the way you're likely to behave. That's how this culture gets perpetuated.

New officers have to be carefully evaluated once they're out on the streets. Superiors should monitor their abilities at deescalation, people-handling skills, communication abilities, attitude, and cultural sensitivity.

THE ATTITUDE TEST

Blacks know all about the attitude test. It's very simple. When you are in the presence of a police officer, you bow down your head. I don't mean literally—just that in every gesture, tone, and facial movement you show submission. You don't ask why. You don't smirk. You don't look angry. You don't curse. That's because you never know when you're going to be given the attitude test, and if you flunk the test, you're going to get hurt.

It may well be, in this day and age, that the majority of police officers don't give the test anymore. The problem is, you just never know.

The most explosive situations occur when you have a black man with a real attitude confronted by a police officer on a big power trip. I once represented Mr. Attitude himself—Tupac Shakur. This was in 1991, when Tupac was just starting to really hit it big. Fame and money didn't sit that well on Tupac's shoulders, in my opinion. They added an edge to an already edgy soul. In the end, fame and money might have killed him.

One thing Tupac had right, however, was that he wasn't *required* to show respect to anyone who treated him with disrespect. He wasn't about to bow down his head.

On this particular day, Tupac was rushing out of a bank in downtown Oakland. As he crossed the street, two officers approached him and cited him for jaywalking. One of the officers was Alexander Boyovich, who had been involved in the Darrell Hampton beating.

Almost the first words out of the officers' mouths were sarcastic. They told Tupac that he might be a member of a rap group, a star, but he'd better know his place in Oakland. He wasn't above the law. One of the officers added, "I can't believe your mother really named you Tupac." Tupac was offended. As he said later, "I told them to give me the ticket, I uttered a profanity and told them that I wasn't a slave, and they weren't my master. One said, 'Hey, I like the sound of that . . . *master.*'"

At that point, Tupac said, "What would you like me to do? Call you 'Your Honors'? By the way, my name really *is* Tupac."

"Okay, Tupac," one of the officers responded. "When you're in Oakland, 'Your Honor' will do just fine."

Tupac was never at a loss for a verbal comeback. More words were exchanged. The officers grabbed Tupac and threw him to the ground, hitting his head on the sidewalk. Then they handcuffed him and took him to jail. Hospital reports revealed that Tupac suffered significant injuries.

Why did this occur? Tupac wasn't respectful enough—he flunked the attitude test, and he happened to be in the presence of two officers who took the test very seriously.

It's always a tough call for me when I have to tell kids what they should do in circumstances like this. I want to empower them, give them a sense of dignity, let them know they have rights. At the same time, I don't want them to end up *dead* right.

Not long ago, I encountered a situation involving a young woman in the Montclair district of Oakland. It's a ritzy, very upper-middle-class area, and she was an eighteen-year-old senior at Skyline High, vice president of the student body, bright, and self-assured.

She and a group of her friends—all from upper-middle-class families, all black, two girls and six boys—were celebrating the birthday of one in the group at a local playground. They were playing basketball, talking, having a good time.

Two police cars drove up at high speed. The cops jumped out, yelling, "Put your hands up!" To the boys, they yelled, "Put your hands behind your backs! Now!"

This girl was a natural leader, and she'd never had any trouble with the police before. Neither had any of the other kids. So she stepped forward and said to the cops, "What did they do? We've been here playing basketball. No one's done anything." One cop said, "Shut up! Put your hands behind your back!"

At this point, she told the other girl to go home and call one of the parents. In the meantime, the police had the boys lined up against a fence. They told them that there had been a purse-snatching in the area, and the suspect had been seen running toward the playground.

Again, the student vice president spoke up. "Well, it certainly wasn't any of these boys. They've been here playing basketball with us for the last couple of hours."

The cop said, "You're being too smart. If you don't shut up, we're going to arrest you."

Her response? "We haven't done anything wrong, and besides, you haven't even read us our rights. Now leave us alone!"

The officers then grabbed her, pulled back her arms, cuffed her, and threw her in the back of the police car. She was arrested on the grounds that she had assaulted a police officer.

I was disgusted after hearing her story when her parents brought her to my office. What kind of an impression had that police action made on this young woman? Bright, articulate, about to go off to college, she'd had her first encounter with the police, and they had violated her civil rights.

"You thought you had rights, didn't you?" I said to her, as she sat across from me, hot with indignation.

The young woman leaned forward and looked me in the eye. "I do have rights, Mr. Burris. I just didn't have any during that particular incident."

I liked her spirit, but in the end I gave her this advice: "Be less challenging. You have rights, but go along with the program until you can talk to a lawyer. You don't want to place yourself in a position where you find yourself at the mercy of a cop who isn't interested in hearing what you have to say. You've got to think, 'This guy isn't listening—and he could hurt me.' It's better to suffer the momentary indignity of obeying someone you think is out of line than to confront them at that moment. As long as there's no physical pain being inflicted, take a deep breath, let it go, and deal with it later. An abusive cop, given the opportunity, will hurt you. I'm very sure about that. Then he'll lie about it, and you'll be placed in a very difficult position.

"You think you've got rights? You do. But you have to know when to apply them, and when to accede to authority in an attempt to get through a potentially threatening situation. Dangerous moments can come when you least expect them. Be ready."

It's the same thing I tell my own kids. It's a conversation I hate to have. But communication is a two-way street. If dialogue is only going one way, it can slam into a brick wall.

Verbal Judo

The Christopher Commission Report on the LAPD noted, as a positive occurrence, that a special eight-hour course, called Verbal Judo, had recently been introduced. Its aim was to teach officers to use verbal skills to avoid having to use force. While I applaud any training effort that limits unnecessary confrontations between cops and citizens, it seems to me that this approach may be part of the problem, not part of the solution.

You might learn a few handy techniques in an eight-hour course. But you won't learn an internal instinct. An eight-hour course on "verbal judo" is ultimately no more effective than an eight-hour course on *physical* judo would be. Judo is a discipline—a training that is so constant and so rigorous as to shift a person's interior mapping. The training evolves into an instinct—a natural reaction in the face of particular circumstances. You show me *that* kind of training in verbal judo, and I'll agree you have something worthwhile.

Most police academy training courses devote more time to writing reports than they do to communication. Even less time is spent on how to relate to different cultural groups, although most urban police forces are composed of a majority of white officers working in multicultural neighborhoods.

In my opinion, mastery of verbal judo would mean something like the following could occur.

You encounter a young black man like Tupac Shakur. He's full of himself and he has little respect for you. You stop him because he's jaywalking, which is a violation of the law. He may sneer at you, even use profanity. You're just doing your job, writing the citation.

You evaluate the situation in an instant, and this is what you conclude:

- Tupac Shakur is not dangerous to you. He's not even interested in you. He's just annoyed at being stopped because he's in a hurry.
- Although he is mouthing off and letting you know just how annoyed he is, Tupac is cooperating. He has given you his driver's license as ID. He's waiting while you write the ticket.

• Jaywalking is on the lowest rung in the ladder of offenses. It's like giving a parking ticket—a combination of keeping the streets clear and earning revenue for the city.

What do you do? You finish writing the ticket. You don't let him bait you into a confrontational discussion. You stay even-tempered and polite. After he signs the ticket, you walk away.

It sounds simple, and it is if you have the training. A police officer's job mostly involves talking to people. All kinds of people. If you take every insult as if it were a jab to the jaw, you'll be punch-drunk before your first day on the job is over.

Here's another situation a police officer may encounter:

Say you get a report that a young black man has just grabbed a woman's purse and witnesses saw him headed for the playground. You drive in that direction, and the first thing you notice is a group of black kids at the playground. You jump out of your car and approach them. What do you observe?

• The kids are older—maybe seventeen or eighteen.
• Two girls are sitting on a bench, talking.
• Four boys are shooting hoops, wearing shorts and T-shirts.
• Everyone looks relaxed, like they're having a good time.
• No one in the group reacts suspiciously when your car pulls up to the playground.

This is the scene you register as you approach the group. Does it square with the furtive movements that would accompany the theft of a woman's purse just moments earlier? Your judgment is that this group is probably not involved in the theft—even though the boys, like the thief, are black.

Since you have made these observations about the group, you do not rush up to them and scream at the boys, "Put your hands up! Put your hands behind your backs. Now!" You have visual control of the scene. You can see that it is safe to approach in a conversational manner.

You tell the kids about the purse-snatching. You ask them if they saw anyone running through the park. You find out who they are. (A question or two would give you the information that these kids live in the neighborhood, attend the school, and are excellent students.)

Having observed and listened, you can reasonably conclude that none of these kids were involved in the robbery. Can you be 100-percent certain? Probably not. Do you have reason to search them? Not really.

If the situation were reversed, and the suspect were white, would you search a group of white kids at the playground? Probably not.

A skilled police officer will evaluate the situation. He will determine what is reasonable.

Verbal judo is the ability to use your senses and your dialogue with the people you encounter, to judge the likelihood of a problem. If your mind is cluttered with racial stereotypes, your own ego, a power trip, fear, or any other distracting factors, you will not be able to make a sound judgment. The failure to communicate is the gravest failure of all. What a shame more time isn't devoted to verbal judo at police academies.

Chapter 11

SKIN SO BLUE

*The most difficult battle to be won against
the enemy in the future must be fought
within ourselves, with an exceptional effort
that will transform our appetite for hatred
into a desire for justice.*

—ALBERT CAMUS

For as long as he could remember, growing up in Orlando, Florida, Derrick Norfleet knew he wanted to be part of the solution, not part of the problem. That's why he joined the Marine Corps at the age of eighteen, and that's why he went to Columbia College. And that, too, was why he set his sights on becoming a police officer.

Sergeant Derrick Norfleet; stepping across the line.

When you see Derrick today, dressed in the casual attire of the community policing division he supervises, you just know this man was born to be a role model for black kids. He's a sergeant now, in the Oakland Police Department. Strong, handsome, intelligent, and committed—he stands tall. More than that, Derrick has courage. I'm not talking about the quality of "bravery" that goes with the territory when you're a cop. This is courage that is harder won than a badge.

Let me tell you a story about Derrick.

UNDERCOVER—AND INVISIBLE

It happened on a night in July 1988—more than ten years ago as I write this. Derrick had been a police officer for four years, and he often volunteered for undercover work with the narcotics unit on his days off. His role was to go to a site where drugs were being dealt, pose as a buyer, then leave the scene, signaling to his partner. A second stakeout team would then sweep down on the location and arrest the sellers.

Derrick always partnered with another young black cop named Ron Davis. Davis and Norfleet had gone through the academy together and had become friends. It was Ron Davis, in fact, who had initially urged Norfleet to join him in undercover work.

Neither Derrick nor Ron Davis were regular members of the Special Duty Units, which focused on the worst neighborhoods for drugs and violent crimes. On this July night, they were assigned to Special Duty Unit 3, working with three regulars: Bernard Thurman, Mike Cefalu, and Tom Chon.

The target was a notorious drug location in a run-down house on 96th Avenue in East Oakland. In recent years, this poor, working-class neighborhood had been infiltrated by slumlords and drug dealers, and police had been fighting an uphill battle against the onslaught. Norfleet went into the house and came out a few minutes later, having made a buy of crack cocaine. He signaled Ron Davis, who then signaled the other waiting officers to make their move.

Following the plan, Norfleet then ran up 96th Avenue and across Sunnyside Street, and cut through Carter Park. Just as he reached the corner of the park, he heard the roar of a familiar engine—the revved-up cars they used for undercover pursuit—and the squealing of tires. He looked behind him, and saw that one of the undercover teams was pursuing him.

Assuming they planned to perform a fake takedown and arrest on him to protect his identity as an undercover officer, Derrick stopped and threw his hands up in the air. He heard the engine behind him accelerate and, just as he started to turn and look again, the car hit him from behind. He was flipped backward and landed on the hood of the police car before rolling off onto the ground. Derrick felt incredible pain in the back of his legs as he slammed down and came to a hard fall on his stomach and face. Before he had a chance to recover and roll over, he heard car doors opening, and the crunch of feet striking earth.

Derrick was still on his stomach when the beating started— he was hammered with fists, kicked repeatedly, and someone

171

crashed a heavy flashlight down on his ankle. Rough hands snapped cuffs on his wrists and turned him over on his back. Through bleary eyes, he saw the forms of the three backup officers—Cefalu, Thurman, and Chon.

"Oh, fuck, this is Norfleet," Thurman said in disgust, as he realized their mistake. He quickly undid the handcuffs. "Hey, we're sorry, man, you know? We thought you were a suspect!"

Chon and Cefalu both apologized, too. "We didn't realize it was you, Derrick. Must've got our signals crossed. You all right?"

"Just put me in the car, okay?" Norfleet said, wincing. At that moment, Ron Davis came running up, yelling, "I told you guys he was my partner. I kept telling you not to bother my partner."

Thurman and Chon helped Norfleet into Davis's undercover car, and then they all returned to the house where Derrick had made the buy, so he could do a field ID on the suspects that had been apprehended.

Norfleet didn't even check himself for bruises. He was mostly concerned about walking, because of the intense pain he was feeling in his legs. After the suspects had been sorted out, he limped around trying to work out the pain in the back of his legs. Sergeant Rivera, the supervisor on the scene, asked him what was wrong, and so Norfleet told him what had happened. Rivera was pissed. He immediately chewed out Cefalu, Thurman, and Chon—especially Cefalu, the driver of the car.

"Do you need an ambulance?" Rivera asked Derrick.

"No," Derrick told him. "I think I can walk it off."

Davis drove him a couple of blocks away and parked, and Derrick got out and walked around for about ten minutes. He had a slight limp, but felt well enough to work the rest of the shift—until four-thirty that morning. At first he switched jobs with Davis, waiting in the car while Ron made the buys. Eventually he grew bored with that and made a couple of buys himself.

By the end of the shift, Derrick felt sore all over, but he still thought he could shake it off. The back of his legs hurt the most, where the car had hit him, and it wasn't until they stopped aching that he noticed his left ankle was very swollen where the heavy flashlight had made contact.

In the end, it would take a couple of weeks for the full extent of Derrick's injuries to show up. His stomach gave him trouble; he felt sharp pains that made him gasp, and he had trouble keeping food down. He noticed his head hurt in a couple of spots, too, and he began suffering from night sweats—and nightmares. They were always the same. It was night, it was dark, and he was being cornered and beaten.

Finally Derrick went to his doctor, and she ran a battery of tests. Although she found nothing conclusive, she cautioned Derrick that stress caused the body to react in many different ways, and he should consider stress as a factor.

On the surface, life went on as normal. Apart from mentioning what had happened to Sergeant Rivera, Derrick had kept quiet. He never made an official report. In the weeks to come, Derrick worked with all of the officers involved in the incident on additional undercover operations, and on routine patrol assignments. In his quiet way, he spoke to each of the officers—not making any accusations, but just trying to find out how this could have happened. It gnawed at him. For Derrick, it wasn't simply a matter of mistaken identity, as all of the officers claimed it to be. What he wanted to know was why they would run *anyone* down that way (and then beat the crap out of him!)—even a suspected drug dealer. *Why?*

Later Derrick would remember Mike Cefalu's response. It was chilling. "Sometimes we hit them with the car to knock them down," he shrugged.

Derrick's physical problems were starting to resolve themselves, but the psychological disturbance intensified. His solid marriage had suddenly turned shaky, and it had all started after the incident on July 12. He just wasn't functioning normally. He was angry at himself, angry at everybody around him, angry at the police department.

"I didn't know who to trust in the department," he would say later, "who to say what to. And it got bad at home, where my wife just said, 'I think you ought to see somebody.' I really believed that I could handle it on my own, but things were starting to break down. I didn't want to come to work. I felt like they had taken something away from me, and I just didn't want to be around anybody. I had sort of withdrawn back into my own little world, and I didn't want anybody to know what had happened."

It wasn't until a month after the incident, when an administrative officer in personnel noticed that an on-the-job injury report hadn't been filled out, that it was brought up again. Whenever a police officer is injured or sick, a form has to be filled out and filed. The officer who handled all of the injury and sick claims sent Derrick an on-the-job injury form from Sergeant Rivera and asked him to fill it out, which he did. He completed the top half of the report, detailing the injuries, leaving the bottom half of the report—Comments, Conclusions, Disposition—blank, for Rivera to fill in.

One night after lineup, the captain called Derrick into his office. "What happened when you worked for the task force? I heard some things." And so, reluctantly, Derrick told the captain—and then it started.

The captain was incensed. He punched his intercom and ordered a transcriber. "I want a written statement," he said. Derrick had tried to avoid this moment, but now it was out of his hands. The chief was notified, and he demanded an investigation by Internal Affairs.

Internal Affairs interviewed Derrick, but he was hoping the matter would drop. He didn't want to be the guy that fingered his fellow officers. He just wanted to forget the whole thing. And yet he didn't. The two compulsions vied with each other inside him, and when the Internal Affairs investigation didn't lead to a resolution, Derrick felt not only personally betrayed by his department, but also shocked that renegade behavior on the part of undercover cops was tacitly allowed. That's not why he became a police officer. Even a drug dealer had rights.

After a lengthy struggle with his conscience, Derrick made a decision that was singularly courageous. He came to me and asked me to file a lawsuit against the city of Oakland and the OPD. From the start, I could see that Derrick found no pleasure in the prospect of a lawsuit. It hurt him to break ranks, and he was well aware that he might be putting a cap on his career.

Derrick's belief in the integrity of police work was in conflict with his sense of who he was as a black man. He couldn't reconcile his fellow officers doing what they did to him, and still see them as good cops. From Derrick's point of view, he had done everything right. If his fellow officers thought he was a perp, okay. He'd play by the rules. Hands up in the air. Submit completely. That was their training. He'd be fine. But when the backup team ran him down, when the officers came out of the car punching and kicking, they had gone over the line. Even if he'd been a drug dealer, even if he'd been a perp, they had gone too far.

From the moment the suit was filed, Derrick became the enemy in the only profession he had ever wanted. He was shunned by the white cops, avoided by old friends like Ron Davis, made the object of derision. It was not uncommon during that difficult period to find derogatory comments slashed on the bathroom walls and in the elevators of the precinct—ugly racial slurs and death threats.

During that period, I came to appreciate the extent of Derrick's courage. He stuck with it, still trying to be the best police officer he could be.

"My belief in God has allowed me to say, 'What's going to happen is going to happen.' " he told me one day. "Whatever happens, I'm going to deal with it." He flashed me his trademark grin. "So, other than that, everything is okay."

Other than *that*.

During the trial, I asked Derrick if he thought the attack was racially motivated. He demurred. "Now, that's a question mark," he answered. "Personally, now, I don't know. I can't say yes or no. I don't know. All I know is what happened to me, and I don't know what the guys were thinking."

I think Derrick's reply represents the dilemma of many Americans. We *want* our society—our coworkers, comrades, colleagues, friends—to see beyond the shallow divide of race. And I realized that Derrick saw himself as being the color of his uniform, not the color of his skin. He was one of them; they were comrades. *Skin so blue.* Maybe that hurt him the most.

The jury ruled against the department in favor of Derrick, regarding the injuries sustained when he was struck by the car. They didn't award him any damages for the beating. "The beating was okay," Derrick says. "I guess they figured that when Cefalu hit me with his car, that was going too far." There is no humor in his laugh.

This is the way I see it: What Officer Derrick Norfleet did constitutes a singular act of courage against overwhelming odds. Did it make a difference? I don't really know. I only know this; Derrick found himself in a position where he had to decide—would he do nothing, or would he step across the line? He stepped across the line. Furthermore, in an even greater act of courage and commitment to the community, he stayed on the force.

So, when I consider whether or not Derrick's act made a difference, I would like to think it did. But I am also aware that a man's courage ultimately may not have much value to anyone else. It's a stand you take, and sometimes the only place it makes a difference is in your own gut.

WALLS AGAINST TRUTH

Derrick Norfleet believed that there was safety in integrity. He was pained beyond words to witness the closing of ranks, the furtive lies, the decision to ostracize him because he spoke the truth. In a sense it was a dual ostracism: first when he was the invisible man, beaten on the ground; and second when he chose to enter a lawsuit against his own. The other police officers never understood that they had not treated him like a colleague that night, yet they demanded that he be one in the aftermath, and lie for them. The unspoken expectation was that Derrick would not speak of what had happened. If pressed, he would minimize. Once he told the truth, the wall closed behind him, and he found himself standing on the outside.

The single most tenacious obstacle to reform in police departments across the nation is what is known as the "blue wall," or the "code of silence." The origins of the code are grounded in the unconditional trust among soldiers—the confidence that no matter what, your colleagues will watch your back. This trust is essential to high-risk pursuits. To perform the daily job of policing, you must be able to trust that your partner, your team, and the department, are in sync with you. A lapse in trust, a moment of hesitation, can be deadly.

Inevitably, those who place their lives on the line become bonded in a manner whose only analogy is war. But it is a false analogy, and a flawed bond. Of course, we are all aware of the argument for the warrior fidelity. It is the strong bond of loyalty and esprit de corps that keeps trained soldiers fighting as a team rather than devolving into individuals under the intense pressures of combat.

The same theory is meant to hold true for the police, and in some very important ways, it does—with this vital difference: The rules of engagement in a combat zone are vastly different from the rules of engagement in a society. When police officers are encouraged to believe that a state of war exists between them and the people, the only result is that lawlessness abounds—on the part of the law enforcers. When a military model is juxtaposed over a civilian society, officers of the law justify extreme actions. Yet even in war there is honor.

To excuse the use of brutality against the innocent by citing the dangers that officers face from criminals is specious. These are the excuses of small minds, of those who can't accept that cops receive their power from the people, not from the butt of a gun. Indeed, in a given year, the majority of police officers never fire their weapons while on duty even once.

It is impossible to fully appreciate, as an outsider, how painfully the code of silence wears on a good cop. We can all stand on the outside and speak righteously about the need for police officers to be truthful, but as long as the police culture itself does not demand an ethical code of honesty, our words mean nothing. I'll tell you why.

Let's say that you're a good police officer who loves your work and does a good job. One day you find yourself in a situation where you observe another officer brutalizing a citizen. Maybe the victim is a guy like Darrell Hampton, who was just trying to do *his* job; maybe it was a Doug Stevens, walking down the street. Let's take it one step further. Say the police officer who is beating up a citizen is your superior officer; he's a sergeant, and you've been out of the academy for only a year.

Do you try to stop the beating? You can try, of course, if you yourself want to be arrested for interfering with an officer. It would put a quick end to your career. Most likely, you swallow your disgust and say nothing.

Later the charges against the citizen are filed: resisting arrest, assault on a police officer, and so on. You know they're not true. When you are asked what happened, what do you say? If you tell the truth, you are taking a stand that has grievous ramifications—not for the brutal officer, but for yourself. Maybe it'll be your word against that of ten other officers. Your word against a sergeant's. You're new on the force and expendable. Others control your fate—and the very sergeant you would be speaking up against is the man responsible for evaluating your performance.

You ask yourself, *Will the truth matter? Will justice be done because* you *speak out?* The bitter truth: No. Those who step forward and break the code rarely, if ever, force any action against brutal officers.

So the real question becomes, Is it worth it to ruin your career in order to achieve *nothing?* Wouldn't it be better to try and fight for change from the inside?

The conclusion of this painful soul-searching will most likely be that you say nothing. You build a justification that allows you to go along with the lie. And the next time, it's easier.

We have to be absolutely clear: This is the setting in which the truth and the lie battle for supremacy.

Truth and Consequences

There was an officer in the Rodney King case whose soul was so raw from this battle, you could see it in his face. In the criminal trial in Simi Valley, Officer Ted Briseno broke the code and testified against his fellow officers. He told the jury that he thought most of the blows were unnecessary and that he had tried to stop the beating at one point. Briseno was not free of fault himself. The videotape shows that he had stomped King on the head with his boot, but he was acquitted of charges in both the first criminal trial and in the federal civil-rights trial.

In the civil trial, I called Briseno to the stand as the first witness. He was clearly a troubled man. His eyes were heavy with sadness, and his demeanor was jittery. It was hard to imagine him as a confident young police officer.

My job was to hold Briseno to his previous testimony. I sensed he was under a great deal of pressure. He had been suspended without pay from the LAPD for the last three years, and I knew he was trying to get his old job back.

Even now, in court, it was plain to see he was being ostracized by the other cops. He and his lawyers sat far away from the other officers and their lawyers. He was not one of the boys. He stood apart.

On the stand, I gazed into his troubled eyes, and I felt some sympathy for him. But when he began to speak, he told an entirely different story than the one he had told before. He explained that he'd had a chance to carefully review the tape, and he realized that only a glancing blow—an accidental swipe—had hit King in the face. He claimed that he had changed his opinion of what happened over a year ago.

I was furious. Briseno had testified before a Board of Rights hearing only a few months ago, and given his original version. Now, I suspected, he was desperate to be accepted back into the force, and he was trying to reset the clock on his life. I declared him a hostile witness and attacked him with a vengeance.

"Is it right that you are trying to tell us you were aware your perceptions may have changed and yet you gave sworn testimony to the contrary in September?" I asked.

Briseno stared back at me with pained eyes. "That's correct," he said. He lowered his eyes and stammered as he searched for words. "If I can help . . ."

I'd had enough. "It's not *me* you need to help," I said bitingly, and I turned away from him. "I'm through with this witness."

Briseno was trying to have it both ways, but that wasn't going to happen. Now he had lost not only his place in the fraternity; he had lost even the fragment of integrity he had maintained in the other trials. He was a tragic man.

During the Mollen Commission hearings in New York City, Detective Jeff Baird, an Internal Affairs investigator, testified about the ways police commanders covered up corruption cases. Was Baird hailed as a hero? No. In the aftermath of his testimony, Baird was denied a promised promotion and transferred from his job. He received death threats—and worse—from other officers. "They told him he was going to be put out on the street for every raid," said Baird's attorney, the late William Kunstler. "And someone else threatened that they would reveal his identity [to drug dealers] and get him killed."

That was in 1994. Today, Baird is still awaiting the outcome of a complaint he filed under the "Whistle-Blower Statute"—a complaint that cops set on retaliation ruined his career, vandalized his office, isolated him, threatened him, and even sent pornography to his five-year-old son.

BREAKING THE CODE

There is only one way to break the code of silence. That is, to make the truth a more appealing alternative than the lie.

When I was writing this book, I spoke with many people— criminal-justice experts, police officials, citizens—and often they expressed private doubts that the blue wall would ever crumble. What conceivable incentive could departments offer that would cause a man or woman to cross the line?

"Every police officer is fully aware of the ramifications," an official who asked to remain nameless told me. "They know it's their responsibility, they know they are bound to uphold the law and do the right thing, but it comes down to whether or not they are willing to risk everything—including the safety and well-being of their families. Because we have not insisted on a fundamental ethical code in our departments, we are asking individual officers to sacrifice themselves—and for what?"

We cannot be naive about what constitutes motivation for a police officer to report instances of misconduct that he or she observes. It is not effective simply to tell officers that they are expected to be truthful. Officers must see examples of the consequences of the lie, and they must see the crumbling of the structure that protects the lie.

For example, in New York City, there is a mandatory 48-hour "cooling off" period for a police officer before he or she is required to give an official statement about an incident. This extraordinary allowance was won by the union, and I am not alone in suggesting that there is only one logical explanation for it—to help officers get their stories straight. In other words, to help them lie. Certainly citizens are not entitled to "cool off" before they are hammered by aggressive questions and made to sign statements.

There must be a clear message from the top, communicated in actions as well as in words, that lying will not be tolerated, and that it will be grounds for dismissal and possibly prosecution. Those at the helm of law enforcement must recognize that untruthful officers jeopardize their efforts to fight crime. A judge in New York City, who sits on the bench in a community that is primary black and Hispanic, told me, "Jurors here will not convict if there is even the slightest hint that a police officer might not be telling the truth."

In 1997, Boston chief judge Robert A. Mulligan established a reporting system under which criminal judges in Suffolk County would report to him monthly any perceived instances of police officers who had lied under oath. Mulligan would then submit a report to the district attorney and the police commissioner, as well as to a defense attorney appointed to be a member of this select task force. The goal is to send a strong warning to officers that there is a no-tolerance policy for lying in court.

When the statements of police officers contradict hard evidence, it must be assumed—by the department and the district attorney's office—that the police officers are lying. Appropriate consequences must follow, both on the departmental and the criminal level.

For example, in the case of Martin Trahan, described in Chapter Seven, the discrepancies between the police officers' version of the moments leading up to his death, and the findings of the autopsy, were in direct conflict. The discrepancy is so clear that an investigation should have been immediately launched.

POLICE OFFICERS— Stated that they did not, at any time, strike Trahan on the head with batons or flashlights.

AUTOPSY REPORT— Two scalp contusions.
Skull crushed and flattened.
Brain smashed and swollen.
A choke hold was not applied.
Five areas of blunt trauma to the neck.
Petechial hemorrhaging.
Pulmonary edema.
Extreme swelling in the lungs and trachea.

In the wake of a massive corruption scandal in New York City, which led to the dismissal of 125 criminal cases because of police prevarication, the department has started including extensive training in the police academy about the consequences of perjury, and how to avoid it. In one segment, officers are asked to role play a scene in which they are made to choose between lying to protect their partner, or telling the truth. Cadets are repeatedly told that lying is not worth it; it will cost them their jobs, their pensions, and their self-respect.

While these are steps in the right direction, we can't pretend that the code will be broken so easily.

There is an image from a newspaper article that stays in my mind—a moment that was described as having taken place in the Seventieth Precinct station house in New York City; four months earlier, several cops from that precinct were accused of the supremely brutal attack on Abner Louima, a Haitian man, in the bathroom of the station—an attack that was said to include sodomy with a toilet plunger. On this day, one of the officers accused in the grisly incident walked into the station for the first time since the incident, and received a hero's welcome. A line of blue formed—offering him handshakes, pats on the back, hugs, and words of support. His lawyer stood to the side and watched, smiling broadly. "He's like the messiah in this precinct," he said.

Chapter 12

THE PARTNERSHIP

*Every honest man will suppose honest acts
to flow from honest principles.*
—THOMAS JEFFERSON

The nation's top law-enforcement officials all agree that the most effective way to reduce the conflict between police and citizens is through a commitment to community policing.

According to the Office of Community Oriented Policing Services (COPS), which was created by the Department of Justice in 1994, community policing can serve two vital purposes:

1. It helps to reduce both crime and the fear of crime.
2. It rebuilds the bond between the police and the people they serve.

That bond, as we know, has been severely frayed, especially in minority communities. It has taken far too long for law-enforcement officials to acknowledge that, to a great extent, their own tactics have exacerbated tensions and, in effect, sabotaged their crime-fighting efforts. Crime is a complex problem that cannot be solved by dollars and brute force. Local people, who have the most at stake when it comes to ridding their communities of crime (for *they*, not some abstract mass, are its victims), must be viewed as partners, not impediments.

Today there are numerous programs that have been created for the express purpose of bringing the community, and the police departments that serve them, closer together. Photos and articles appear regularly in the local newspapers, extolling a community police officer's appearance at a nearby elementary school or senior citizens' center, giving or receiving a plaque, presenting crime-prevention tips or drug-education and awareness awards. This visibility and interaction go a long way toward making the citizens in these communities feel as though there really *is* someone they know in the police department, and it's all for the good.

WHAT IS COMMUNITY POLICING?

According to COPS, the tenets of community policing involve active engagement with the day-to-day lives of the citizens.

For example, individual officers might go into the neighborhoods, walk the beat, talk to people, develop relationships, become familiar, find out what's going on. Is anybody having any problems? It could be anything—the idea is that the police are able to do a lot more than arrest drug dealers and snoop around, give tickets, and behave in an authoritarian, punitive way.

Community policing officers can be there to help out; to facilitate for citizens with the often-confusing bureaucracy of other city agencies; to listen to people's problems, act as a communications link between themselves and the department; develop relationships that can place them in a position of mediation if the need ever arises. Secondarily, developing these relationships among the community and the department can lead to direct access to information if trouble strikes or a crime is committed—a rape, a burglary, a robbery, or a murder.

It goes without saying that community policing is done within the parameters of a hostile relationship developed from notorious past behavior on the part of police in many of these communities. As such, it is not easy to break through the barriers of cynicism and distrust. However, community policing can reduce the very real tensions that exist between the police and the neighborhoods that they patrol. For example, there may be a situation where people in the community complain to "their" officer about the behavior of another officer. It remains to be seen whether the community policing officer can or will do anything about it, but it's vital that those kinds of informational links are maintained. Of course, the more stock you put in community policing, the more resources are going to be directed there, and the more effective it can be.

MIXED MESSAGES

Community policing has no chance of working when it is viewed as an ancillary effort. Its principles must pervade the department. If a small group of officers is engaged in community policing, while many others are walking the streets behaving like an occupying force, it's not going to work.

For example, Darrell Hampton worked closely with community policing officers in his position as director of the Acorn Housing Project Community Center. He organized events for his kids with police officers, and participated in PAL. As he himself says, "I was 'Mr. Police.' "

But on the day that Darrell Hampton crossed paths with Officer Mike Yoell and his fellow officers, it made no difference whatsoever. That one incident, in front of innumerable witnesses—most of them children—left an indelible imprint that simply wiped away all of the years of relationship-building.

The dichotomy of community policing is that it doesn't offer a "quick fix." And let's face it, a quick fix, a speedy "War on Crime," is the highly touted goal of American law-enforcement agencies. However, community policing requires a long-term commitment on the parts of the police department, the local government, and the people who are being policed. Patience, time, and a gradual change in attitude is what makes it work, and that's sometimes a difficult perspective to keep, on the parts of both citizens and police.

Given the slow crawl of true change, it is difficult for many departments to make their community policing programs a priority, or to fully integrate them into the mainstream of their departments. Precious manpower and economic resources are being diverted to community policing programs, when many police chiefs think that the bulk of resources should be directed to proactive law enforcement—drug task forces, undercover operations, hiring of more personnel, more equipment, more vehicles, more video surveillance systems.

Although many law-enforcement experts believe that enforcement itself is not going to fully resolve the toughest crime problems—witness the failure of the War on Drugs—there is a national dread of being perceived as being "soft" on crime. You can see this in the election rhetoric of our representatives, and you can see it in the emphasis on proactive law enforcement in city governments and police departments. It's the difference between short- and long-term thinking. A big drug bust gives immediate gratification. There is pride and back-slapping, a televised press conference. But when the klieg lights go off, is the community a better, safer place to live? Is there a noticeable improvement? It seems logical that enforcement must be balanced with a supportive environment focused on long-term change.

Community policing is an arm of law enforcement that is also committed to the reduction of crime—but the tactics are different. For example, a community police officer will recognize that it is just as important to know who the good people in a community are, as it is to know the identities of the criminal element. Working-class, law-abiding citizens are the cornerstone of *every* community—no matter how disadvantaged. When the police fail to understand this, and do not acknowledge the solid citizens, it creates a breakdown that is hard to mend.

On a practical level, the community policing officers can figure out who the players are, and who the players aren't. Now, that's a very important function. Where you have task-force units getting ready to knock down doors and pull raids, a word or two with the community officer can straighten out mistaken warrants before any damage is done.

Most of the people in poor neighborhoods live there because of social and economic conditions. They live there because that's where they were born and raised. That's where their families are. That's what they know. It doesn't automatically brand them as criminals. Most of the crime, in fact, is perpetrated against them. On the scale of things, they represent the gazelles grazing on the veldt—the criminal element are the predators who feed on the gazelles. Community police officers can help distinguish between the gazelles and their predators.

A GOOD CITIZEN

Whenever I think about community policing, my thoughts turn to a woman named Barbara Dean. A school psychologist in her forties, Barbara is imbued with a stately, even regal, stature and demeanor. Although she lives in a poor working-class neighborhood in East Oakland, she does so by choice, not necessity. Barbara has a deeply-felt commitment to the improvement of her neighborhood.

Which is why, one afternoon, after she had finished her daily jog around the Arroyo Viejo Park, she was picking up cans and bottles that littered the area. For five years she had been picking up cans and bottles and depositing them in recycling bins. It was a small gesture, a symbol of her hopes for the neighborhood.

On the afternoon of June 1, 1990, as she stopped to pick up some discarded cans, she noticed that several cops were talking to a group of young men who were drinking beer and playing music at a cul-de-sac in the park. Two police cars and an unmarked white van were pulled up near the group. One of the young men had been handcuffed and was being placed in the van.

Barbara Dean; her devotion to the community has never wavered, in spite of her painful experience.

The neighbors all knew Barbara, and knew she picked up cans and bottles for recycling. Several of the teenagers called out to her that they had cans for her to recycle. When she came over, one of the young men poured the remaining beer out of a can and handed it to her. Then a policeman, Officer Sweeney, came up and asked Barbara, "Are you on probation?"

Barbara was caught off guard, shocked by this question and its presumption that she had a criminal record. "Am I on probation?" she repeated. "Why are you asking me this? I've done nothing wrong."

Officer Sweeney responded by ordering her to get into the police van. Barbara was indignant, and frankly, she had a right to be. Who was this bully, ordering her, a dedicated professional and a respected member of the community, into a police van? Who was he to assume that because she was black, she must be on probation?

She refused. "You're making a mistake. I've broken no law."

Without pausing to consider, Sweeney grabbed Barbara around the neck and placed her in a chokehold. He did this so swiftly, and with such force, that Barbara could barely breathe. She was suddenly fearful for her life. What moments before had been a terse conversation, had escalated swiftly and inexplicably into a serious confrontation. The crowd of teenagers stood frozen as Sweeney dragged Dean to the van, slammed her against it, and then handcuffed her.

Barbara did not resist arrest, but again told Sweeney that he had made a mistake, that she was a school psychologist, and that she had two master's degrees in counseling and psychology. She kept expecting Sweeney to hear her, and to acknowledge who she was. But it gradually became clear that he did not view Barbara the way she saw herself, but rather, through some inexplicable distortion, as a neighborhood lowlife, a criminal.

At the police station, as she was booked and her mug shot taken, Barbara continued to expect that she would be quickly released, that somehow this mistake would be rectified, that someone would rush in and say, "Oh, this is *Barbara Dean*. Of course! We're sorry." But, as the hours ticked by, this did not happen. When she finally realized that she was spending the night in jail, she broke down and cried.

Barbara Dean's suit against the Department was settled,

but there is a larger issue. What happened to Barbara Dean is a classic example of an absence of community policing. A well-known, well-respected woman in a community struggling to make itself whole. A woman every police officer on patrol should have known and acknowledged. And because they didn't know her, didn't understand the community culture and its people, a rush to judgment injured Barbara and every person who observed the incident.

The essence of successful community policing is communication, understanding cultural nuances, a willingness to engage with people, a willingness to remain nonthreatening. If any hostility is shown, if there's a sort of on/off switch between being the community policing cop and the hard-nosed cop, then it probably won't work.

It has to be seen as part of the mainstream of police departments, just one of many units—with an equal commitment given to it by the officers assigned to it. It also has to be viewed as a desirable assignment within each department, an assignment that has the possibility of promotion and reward attached to it, so that more-ambitious officers won't be put off by being assigned that duty. An effective community policing officer can serve as a role model for other officers. He or she can be the catalyst for understanding, so that women like Barbara Dean are able to make the positive difference they strive for.

It is a tribute to her strength and decency that Barbara has, in the years since the incident, attempted to use her painful encounter as a springboard for understanding; she has tried to share her experience with children in order to help them deal with their encounters with the police. She can do this because she knows that one bad incident can cripple all efforts for positive change, and she won't let that happen.

"I'll tell you what it did for me," she told me recently. "My faith in God. It was the grace of God that protected me. My degrees, my community service, being who I was—none of that served to help me at the time. It was through the grace of God that I didn't end up being a statistic somewhere. I rely on that more now, trusting in God and having faith that He is the one that will protect us."

SUCCESS STORIES

Community policing can work, but it has to be thoroughly enmeshed within the framework of the departments that institute the program. The Police Athletic League, and all the other worthwhile programs instituted by the police in conjunction with religious and community organizations, are wonderful. But effective community policing relies on training and support from both within and outside of the department. Here are some examples.

• *Chicago, Illinois.* The third-largest city in the nation has the same problems as many other cities—a persistent criminal element. In 1993, the CAPS "beat teams" were formed. Chicago's Alternative Policing Strategy (CAPS) reorganized the department into small geographical areas, where "beat teams" worked with the community members to solve long-term problems.

For example, two gangs had been harassing high-school

students at a bus stop near their school, and the harassment had culminated with the shooting death of a student. At the regular "beat" meeting, cops, residents, and school officials formed a plan. First, the school would stagger the release of students so that smaller groups were gathered at the bus stops. Second, the beat cops in the area would do their daily paperwork in a squad car near the bus stop to establish a police presence.

In another "beat" neighborhood, residents were fed up with gang members and panhandlers. They collaborated on a community-wide effort. Armed only with flashlights, cellular phones, and notepads, groups of citizens walked the streets at night to create a "sphere of safety." Community activists also worked with police to ensure community members were present at all court hearings for people arrested in their neighborhood.

The CAPS program began as an experiment in five areas. It worked so well that Chicago is expanding its community policing program to 279 police beats that blanket the entire city.

- *El Paso, Texas.* The police department in El Paso has decentralized as part of its strategy of making community policing citywide. It has five "regional command centers," each of which is a full-service police department, but located in an area which makes it more accessible to the community. Special Police Area Resident (PAR) officers focus on putting an end to any recurring incidents, and citizen advisory boards have been set up and are regularly consulted to help establish priorities and solve problems that may be plaguing their particular area.

El Paso police are also experimenting with a Citizens On Patrol (COPS) program that teams citizen volunteers with police officers, to walk neighborhood beats together. By patrolling together, the volunteers can learn more about the problems facing the police, and their limitations, while the police can be taught about what's going on by the people who know best—the residents.

Community policing has evolved from local efforts, to those with a national focus. The Community Policing Consortium is a federal community policing initiative created and funded by the Department of Justice. Begun in 1993, it focuses on the aims of community policing and offers information about how to establish programs and apply for a federal COPS grant.

The Consortium's primary goal is to deliver community-policing training and technical assistance to police departments and sheriff's offices across the nation that are designated COPS grantees.

PERSPECTIVE—DERRICK NORFLEET

Derrick Norfleet, the police officer run down from behind and beaten by his fellow officers during a buy-and-bust operation gone wrong, is still a member of the Oakland Police Department. He's risen to the rank of sergeant, and has been made a supervisor of a community policing division of the department.

Recently I visited with Derrick in the community. He was

dressed in shorts and a tank top, preparing for a ball game with a group of local kids.

When Derrick joined the Oakland Police Department, his goal was to help people. Now, he believes, he's accomplishing something very important. I expressed the concern that I've heard murmured about in the community—that the community policing units are seen as infiltration units, as the eyes and ears of the Special Duty Units in high-crime areas.

Derrick answered with a smile and a laugh. "Our only similarity is in our uniforms, which are styled like jumpsuits. But our work is totally different, John. We get information directly from the community we're serving, and we work on the issues that the community wants us to work on. We're not there like some secret gestapo unit, trying to pick up information. We want to make the community work."

"Does community policing work?" I asked.

"Yes, it can work. It works in the area where people have gotten a little more trusting of the police. In those instances, we have people who are willing to come forward and give us information to help us figure out what's going on in a particular instance. Once they see that we're in it for *them* and we're trying to work for *them*, resolve some of the community issues, it makes it a little easier."

I mentioned to Derrick that I thought many people had trouble understanding the difference between community policing units and the other units that specialize in crime and drug control.

"We have to show them that we're sincere and committed," Derrick responded. *"Telling* them is meaningless. It's just blowing hot air. So we go out in the community, listen to people, try to get input. We say, 'Help us out. If we don't know something bad is going on, point it out to us. If you have criminal activity happening in your building or next door, and you're afraid for your own safety, we'll handle it. But we have to know.' We go to meetings with various community groups, listen to their complaints, their suggestions, their advice, and we try to apply what we're learning."

Derrick and I discussed one of the primary goals of community policing, as stated by national organizations such as COPS. That is, the reduction of crime and fear. Derrick told me that in his experience, community policing helps reduce crime. "It's the people who live in these communities who know what's going on, who see and hear things we never do. We don't have all the answers, and we're open to being taught about what's going on. Take any street corner in Oakland. Four houses sitting on that corner. A shooting takes place, a drive-by or some kind of loud fight. People who live there may have seen who did it, what kind of car it was, how many people, all kinds of information that will help us solve this shooting.

"Typically the police are going to have to come in and start from scratch. We talk to the victim—let's say for the sake of argument that he's a gang member, so he's not going to be forthcoming about what happened. At this point, we're usually left standing around scratching our heads.

"It's different with community policing. When we investigate something that's gone down in our neighborhood, we know the people, we know the particular circumstances surrounding the neighborhood. We walk these neighborhoods—

we ride bikes around here. We go to meetings, picnics; where the community invites us, we go. If something happens, people will talk to us."

"Do the young people talk to you, too, Derrick?" I wondered. "Isn't dealing with the youth a big part of community policing?"

Derrick looked thoughtful. "It's probably the most important thing that we do. We're trying to get a message out: 'We know what happened in the past. We can't change what happened. But we can try to move forward, we can try to learn and grow, we can try to become real people in the course of performing our duties.' "

"How do you go about doing that?" I asked.

"We're trying to show the kids growing up right now that we're just people, just humans like them. They have to be able to see us as more than just police—see that we have families, we have children, we have to deal with a lot of the same issues they have to deal with. No one's pretending any of this is easy. We're out there talking to these kids on the street, instead of 'harassing them,' or arresting them all the time. I come up to groups of kids hanging out, and I talk to them.

"More than that, I have something to offer to these kids. I'm willing to go a long way to make this work. I tell them about some of the programs we've set up. There are programs that these young people can go to, doesn't cost them a nickel, free lunches, sports, all kinds of things. We also have a job-training program set up, and we help some of the kids to get work. Not bad, huh?"

Derrick made a strong point of adding that community policing works only if the community is committed. Police can't enforce it; it has to be cultivated. "The biggest commitment has to be from the community," he said. "And I don't mean that in some abstract sense of 'the community.' I mean everybody—single mothers, parents, kids, schools, the churches, everybody—has to get involved for it to work. When all of them, as a community, say to us, 'We don't want that here—get rid of this problem for us,' and then we do, we're showing them we're no longer self-directed in terms of what we have to offer them. We want to know what they think the problems are. We want to be held accountable. If a call comes in to us, and we don't return it, we're subject to discipline by the department. You didn't know that, right? We added an additional prod, just in case there's ever a problem. I think that's fair.

"We want the community to know that we think of this as a partnership between the two of us—the police and the neighborhood. And we're dedicated to keeping our end of the deal. We want the young people growing up in that neighborhood to have a completely different sense of who we are as police officers—what we do, and how we do it. That's what community policing is about. Changing stereotypes, breaking down myths, and reintroducing police as individuals, as people who happen to keep law and order in your neighborhood. Our presence should be comforting rather than confrontational or hostile."

Chapter 13

THE MAKING OF A GOOD COP

People become house builders through building houses, harp players through playing the harp. We grow to be just by doing things which are just.

—ARISTOTLE

One day a couple of years ago, after representing more than 400 people in cases against police officers, I decided to do a small, unscientific study. I made a list of five officers I had run up against a number of times—men I thought had particular problems relating to the community. These were the bully boys, the cops who swaggered and threatened, the cops whose idea of having a conversation with a black person was swinging a baton or yanking on handcuffs.

I think the nation caught a glimpse of this kind of cop when they watched Mark Fuhrman testify in the O. J. Simpson trial. There is a quality in the face, in the eyes. It's hard to define, but if you're black you recognize it right away. In his book about the case, *In Contempt*, Christopher Darden recalls that the first time he set eyes on Mark Fuhrman, "I had the urge to run.... There was something about this guy..."

What was it? I wondered. What do the repeat offenders, the inherently bad cops, have in common? I thought if I could find out, I might gain insight about how to avoid a high percentage of the brutality that afflicted blacks.

I built my list from the files of five policemen, and I have to say that what I found didn't surprise me.

- Not one of the five men grew up in an urban environment. All were from small towns or suburban communities that were primarily white.
- Not one of the five men had a formal education beyond high school. Three joined the military when they were eighteen, and came into the department as soon as they were discharged. One worked on his father's farm for a couple of years after high school before taking the police exam; another was a construction worker after high school.
- Not one of the five men's parents had a formal education beyond high school.
- All of the men were young when they joined the police force—between twenty and twenty-three.

A pattern began to emerge. It seemed clear.

What is the inevitable result when you take a young kid out of a relatively isolated environment, with little education or sophistication, place him in a military setting for a couple of years, then give him a gun and assign him to a minority neighborhood in an American city?

My conclusion? The pattern of abuse stretched back to recruitment. Of course, I am not the first person to ever suggest this. But, as obvious as the fact seems to some of us, that's how difficult it is for the institution to grasp. While I was writing this book, I read an article decrying the fact that New York City had decided to elevate its recruitment standards. In 1996, when New York raised the bar from twenty to twenty-two years old, and from a high-school diploma to sixty college credits, there were loud protests. When the number of new recruits plummeted, many people said you couldn't attract enough recruits if you required so much.

It occurred to me that if all departments began requiring higher standards, there might well be a period of discomfort, when recruits were not as plentiful. But I also believed that the depletion would correct itself—upward.

The elements of youth, lack of higher education, and social inexperience do not manifest themselves only in aggression. Fear is equally dangerous.

In 1995, I took the deposition of a young Oakland police officer who had been involved in two shootings in the course of two years—one, a teenage boy; the other, a woman. Both were black, both were unarmed, and neither had presented any actual danger to the officer or to others. As I spoke with this young man, I didn't get the impression that he was hostile or overly aggressive. What had happened?

I found my answer in the details of his history. He had grown up in a small town, amid the vineyards of Northern California. There were two blacks in his entire town. He had visited San Francisco a total of four times in his life, and had never crossed the bridge into Oakland.

He had always wanted to be a cop, and after academy he was assigned to patrol in a busy precinct in West Oakland. He had never experienced anything like it in his life.

When he told me that both shootings were accidents, I believed him. He said he didn't know what happened. Things got confusing. The truth, which he never acknowledged directly, was that he was just plain scared. He saw danger on every doorstep; a group of boys walking down the street was a gang; there were no friends, only foes.

He was dismissed from the department after the second shooting, but I was angry. That young man was no more qualified to be an urban police officer than was a man from the moon. He was a danger to the community.

Background assessments of recruits need to be far more rigorous than they have been in the past. They need to delve to deeper levels; the definition of "fit" must be expanded. In the past, our ideas about what type of personality was best suited for police work tended to favor boldness, physical condition, skill with weapons, and the willingness to be proactive in crime control. These criteria are certainly necessary, but their emphasis, to the exclusion of all other qualities, has left most cities with police forces that excel in force and are ill-equipped for mental combat.

In my experience, higher education is the most decisive element that differentiates a well-balanced police officer from one who cannot maneuver comfortably in a complex urban environment. I am not referring to a couple of classes in junior college, but to a sustained period of schooling. It is not just the "book learning" that occurs in college that makes the difference. It is the socialization—the living, breathing interaction with people from a variety of races, cultures, backgrounds, and beliefs. You might argue that this same encounter with diversity occurs in the military, but there is no comparison. The military is a highly structured, even rigid, environment, narrowly focused on a set of principles that do not apply to everyday civilian life.

Another important part of the qualification process should be to evaluate the kind of person who is applying. Departments tend to view the "character" question narrowly. For example, they may look into an applicant's history regarding controlled substances—an automatic disqualifer—but fail to note a history of domestic violence.

We are only now becoming truly aware of the prevalence of domestic violence in America. It is a very complicated issue. However, some police departments are beginning to note a correlation between the worldview of a spouse abuser and the worldview of a violent cop. Both are grounded in the need for control and domination. Both disdain communication in favor of force. Both operate as enforcer, judge, and jury. A man or woman who uses violence as a means of controlling a partner or children has no place in a police department.

It should also be noted when there is a family history of alcoholism, drug abuse, or domestic violence. These can have an impact on a person's attitudes as well. As a general rule, such background inquires are never made.

No More Cowboys

I'd like to suggest a new attitude test—one for police officers. There's a common thread to many of the cases I handle. Most of the confrontations that occur can be traced to what I call a "cowboy" mentality on the part of the cops involved. They're still playing at being adults, and the game has the same rules it did when they were ten years old playing cowboys and Indians in the backyard.

A cowboy is someone who goes into a black neighborhood and refuses to respect the black man's manhood, the black person's humanity. That is why so many of the conflicts occur between young white cops and young black citizens. There is a fundamental challenge to manhood—and a cowboy is always going to take the bait.

The Race Card

It's not always easy to detect racial prejudice, but you *can* detect ignorance of racial and ethnic differences. You can be aware of the implications of inexperience and a lack of exposure to diverse populations. For example, a person who has no experience in a poor black community might have a tendency to treat all residents with suspicion, thinking poor blacks are prone to crime and violence. He or she might think that their speaking pattern, their slang, the way they relate on the street, is a sign of disrespect. He or she might mistake the steely face of pride for a dismissal of authority. These and other assumptions can be explosive.

Furthermore, if an officer doesn't have experience with people on welfare, families with domestic problems, or large, extended families living in crowded quarters, he or she might be judgmental. If the only screen he or she possesses through which to view a valid lifestyle is a classic nuclear family, there will be a conflict between an idea of what's normal, and an observation of what's real. And that conflict is not going to come out in favor of the community.

How do recruiters ferret out racial prejudices that linger beneath the surface? Long ago, I developed a questionnaire to determine the same things of the juries who would be judging my clients. Perhaps some of the questions would be relevant in a recruitment interview.

- How was race explained to you as a child?
- What messages did your parents communicate to you about race issues?
- How does this differ from how you communicate with your children about race issues?
- What are your most basic fears about race?
- What has been your contact or experience with persons of other races—neighborhood, work, school, church, etc.?
- According to a national Gallup poll, many whites believe that blacks are less intelligent than whites. Do you believe there is any truth to that? If so, what experiences have you had to cause you to feel that way?
- According to the same Gallup poll, many whites believe that blacks tend to stay on welfare longer than others. Do you share a similar view? If so, why?

- Do you believe that blacks tend to break the law more than other groups?
- Have you ever been in an environment—such as work, school, social, church, etc.—where an acquaintance was accused of racial discrimination, or was claiming to be the victim of racial discrimination? If so, describe the circumstances and how you felt.

These questions are certainly not exhaustive, but they can offer some insight into a person's frame of mind. I've used "blacks" in this sample, but departments should include other racial minorities that make up the population, as well as religious groups (such as Hasidic Jews) and homosexuals. It can also be helpful to use current local events involving conflicts with minorities as points of discussion.

The Multicultural Cop

Back in the 1960s, the Oakland Police Department used to place ads in Southern newspapers to recruit a particular style of cop. At that time, to place a young Southern white cop in an urban environment was like throwing kerosene on a raging fire. Times have changed. However, departments need to be vigilant about maintaining an atmosphere of *absolute intolerance* to racial stereotyping.

That intolerance starts in the same way as it starts in the home or in the school—with language. In the Christopher Commission's report on the LAPD, investigators noted a blatant and frequent usage of racial slurs when officers communicated with one another over patrol-car radios or computers. It was natural—part of the lingo.

Shortly before the Rodney King beating, Officers Powell and Wind, who were among those charged in the incident, radioed a message about a just-completed call to a domestic dispute between an African-American couple, calling it "right out of *Gorillas in the Mist*."

The report also cited other transmitted comments from patrol cars over a period of time, such as,

"Sounds like monkey-slapping time."
"Tell them to go back to Mexico."
"We're huntin' wabbits—actually, Muslim wabbits."

and coded language for profile stops on the freeway:

"U can C the color of the interior of the veh. . . ."
"Ya stop cars with blk interior."
"Negrohyde."

The mentality that pervades departments is that "boy will be boys." Letting off steam in rough neighborhoods contributes to a climate of excessive force. Words matter. Departments must be rigorous in sanctioning officers who use racial slurs in any context.

Departments should view the mannerisms of officers in the same way that corporations view the mannerisms of their employees. It would be hard to find two people standing by the water cooler making racially offensive comments in any American company today. There is zero tolerance—and it comes from the highest court in the land. Surely our law-enforcement officers should be held to the same, if not a higher, standard.

Another way departments can begin to instill sensitivity and understanding into officers who patrol the streets every day, is to establish forums for them to discuss controversial incidents that are occurring right in their precincts. For example, what do you think the result would be if, once a week, roll call started half an hour early and officers were asked to dissect one incident from the previous week in which force was used? For example, say the case up for discussion was the arrest of Marguerite Martin, or the death of Martin Trahan. Officers would be encouraged to give their opinions about what went wrong, what they would have done differently, what options existed other than force, what assumptions were made that were incorrect. If, for thirty minutes every week, the precinct became a classroom, and the discussion remained confidential, imagine the possibilities.

These ideas focus on the interior lives of the men and women who police our streets. Creative minds, with a true will for change, can always elevate their environment.

However, creativity, sensitivity, training, character—none of these will suffice without substantive reform on every level. True reform can be achieved only by a hard-and-fast adherence to a new set of rules. The police departments of America must be rebuilt, from the ground up, using a fresh blueprint.

Here is that blueprint.

Chapter 14

A BLUEPRINT FOR POLICE REFORM

The status quo has never been our god, and we ask no one else to bow down before it.
—CARL T. ROWAN

There was a time when I would have said that change must come from the heart before it can be manifested on the street. In a fundamental sense, that is true. However, over the years, as I've struggled to understand and force change within the institutions of law enforcement, I have come to a more complex realization. It is this: What lives in the heart of a man or woman, is planted by the culture in which they are immersed. And if the heart of a culture is corrupt or indifferent or biased, the hearts of its members will be swayed in that direction. On the other hand, if the heart of a culture is open, fair, and respectful, that seed will take root and, eventually, will grow in all of its members.

If law enforcement is to abandon the culture that supports misconduct, silence, heavy-handedness, and disrespect, a new scaffold must be erected to replace the old. It must be comprehensive, detailed, unwavering, and practical—and it must come from within.

It is my position that if every police department instituted the following 10-point blueprint—aggressively and consistently—it would result in tangible reform within three years' time.

1. Institute a three-tier recruitment standard.

PREMISE: An effective police force must be composed of individuals who have the mentality, experience, and ability to relate to diverse communities and make critical judgments.

Tier 1 will involve basic qualifications for selection—education level, physical-fitness level, and the psychological capabilities necessary to handle the stresses particular to police work. The minimum of a two-year college degree should be a standard, with the requirement waived only on condition that the applicant picks up the degree within a specified period of time. Paid tuition programs are a good incentive, as are higher wages for officers with college degrees. Promotion should also require increased levels of education for each rank.

Tier 2 (for urban police departments) will require life experience in urban areas, work and living experience with ethnic and minority populations, and a demonstrated sensitivity to issues specific to urban populations.

Tier 3 will involve psychological testing and background information addressing the following:

a) any history of violence—domestic or otherwise;

b) negotiation and problem-solving skills;

c) mental and emotional health, temperament;

d) use of alcohol and/or drugs;

e) racial, ethnic, or sexual prejudices;

f) family and community stability;

g) motivations for seeking a career in law enforcement.

2. Establish a dual-training focus of force and communication.

PREMISE: Police officers require extensive training in the use of force, as well as the ability to implement nonviolent, problem-solving skills. These are equally critical to the optimum functioning of police officers in the communities they serve. The critical need to teach *effective communication skills* cannot be stated often enough. It is the key to good policing. When misunderstanding or fear influence the interaction of the police with the community, force is usually substituted for reason.

• Trainees will participate in extensive situational role-playing exercises, designed to teach communication skills and appropriate alternatives to force.

- Special emphasis will be placed on learning and internalizing the continuum of force so that it becomes an automatic procedure.

- A special component focusing on mental and emotional illness is also critically needed as a part of the training—and retraining—of police officers. Many of the walking wounded, released to wander in our society because of the deinstitutionalization of the nation's mentally ill, end up being shot or mishandled because of our current mental-health policies. Police officers are usually the first people who are going to be called if violent, erratic, or otherwise dangerous behavior is being exhibited. It would serve them well to have an extensive understanding of what they might be facing. Mental illness, alcoholism, drug addiction, all seem to be intricately drawn together. It is that multiple interaction of behaviors, symptoms, and reactions that must be quickly assessed by police officers responding to a call, so that they can make decisions based on a clear understanding of the situation.

3. Grade field training on deescalation skills.

PREMISE: In order to pass field probation, an officer must show an ability to deescalate potentially explosive situations.

- Field training officers will seek out opportunities for new officers to use verbal problem-solving skills to deescalate such situations.
- New officers will be graded on their ability to deescalate situations. Deescalation is probably the most crucial skill of

all, and must supplant the macho police reaction to any perceived challenge to authority, which so often escalates into a far more serious and major confrontation than was initially necessary. New officers will also be graded on how well they apply and use force when it is necessary.

- Field training officers will be carefully selected, based on their demonstrated problem-solving abilities and excellent records in relation to the community. They will not have records of citizen complaints in those areas that are vital to teaching communications skills and community relations. In other words, they will be role models. The FTO is the most important link in the process of socialization into the policing culture, so their selection and training is vital to producing solidly trained, ethically sound young police officers. Education is again an important component, and the FTO must use his or her position to reinforce the focus on ethical, reasoned decision-making.

4. Rotate new officers through community policing divisions.

PREMISE: Community policing is essential probationary experience.

- A substantial period of a new officer's probationary period will be spent working in a community policing unit.
- All policing should be community-based. A recruit who is only rotating through a unit dedicated to community policing may foster the attitude of having to temporarily perform a period of "social work" until allowed to return to "real" police work.

217

5. Deny promotions to officers with numerous citizen complaints.

PREMISE: An effective police officer is one who is able to use his authority in a manner that inspires confidence in the community in which he works.

- An officer may not be promoted if he or she has three or more sustained citizen complaints within a two-year period. In these circumstances, the officer will not be eligible for promotion for a period of three years after the last complaint, and only if no further sustained complaints occur.
- Every police officer's annual evaluation will include an analysis of complaints, whether sustained or not, and this analysis will be a significant factor in the officer's rating.
- If a police officer is the defendant in a civil-liability suit filed by a citizen that results in a monetary judgment or settlement by the department, this "cost" will factor negatively in considering a promotion.
- Officers who generate numerous citizen complaints should be removed from service. Removing them would serve three purposes:

  a) It would stand as a clear warning to other officers with similar propensities.
  b) The problem officer would no longer be around to influence others toward similar misconduct.
  c) The problem officer could not use an increase in rank as an excuse for further insupportable behaviors.

- It will be common police policy to treat all litigation as a citizen complaint, and to conduct a thorough internal investigation.
- Each department will set a limit to the number of citizen complaints a police officer can receive within a given time frame before he or she will be dismissed from the force.

6. Establish a committee to review policy and standards.

PREMISE: The introduction of new technologies (such as video cameras mounted in squad cars, stun guns, and chemical suppressant sprays), methods (such as K-9 units, SWAT units, and robotic surveillance), and changes in law (such as search-and-seizure laws), requires an ongoing evaluation and update of departmental regulations. Reviews should be designed to reduce unnecessary injuries. Dog bites, stun guns, and overenthusiastic application of chemical sprays, are particular sources of current abuse that can, for the most part, be prevented.

- The department will create a review committee, composed of officers who have completed special training, technical experts, and a high-level officer appointed by the police commissioner.
- Committee members will participate in law-enforcement conferences, departmental interchange programs, and ongoing studies, to keep apprised of new methods and technologies.

- The committee will meet monthly to discuss issues and make recommendations.
- The committee might also be an excellent forum for discussing the civil-rights abuses that are constantly perpetrated under the banner of the "War on Drugs."
- The committee will monitor the varying success levels of weapons, devices, and methods.
- The committee will organize semi-annual conferences and training sessions in which all officers are required to participate.

7. Create an incentive for officers to report misconduct.

PREMISE: An environment must be established which allows officers to report misconduct by fellow officers without suffering negative consequences.

- The police department will act aggressively to break the "blue wall of silence."
- The message will be frequently reinforced to officers, that their sole obligation is to the rule of law, to the stated objectives of the department, and to the well-being of the community.
- An intense focus on ethics is the only means to internally motivate recruits to think correctly and to resist the customs of past misconduct. Constantly harping on negative sanctions is ultimately counterproductive, and only *coerces* the desired behavior. Instead, what must be instilled is a fundamental belief system in simply doing what is "right"—

always—without a thought to doing otherwise, because it is neither tolerated nor accepted.

· To the extent possible considering the circumstances, reports by officers regarding incidents of misconduct will be treated confidentially.

8. Impose discipline on officers who lie.

PREMISE: Police officers are expected to report incidents accurately and truthfully.

· Officers who are found to be lying, or who are perceived to be lying as a result of a jury verdict against them in a citizen lawsuit, will be fired. Since an officer's credibility as a witness depends upon his sworn oath, and is based on a presumption of the truth, a proven liar can no longer effectively perform as an officer. Lying is the greatest impediment to trust between the police and the community.

9. Replace Internal Affairs with an independent review board.

PREMISE: The evaluation of complaints and potential misconduct must be carried out in an objective manner, by an independent board that gives equal weight to the positions of the police officer and the citizen.

· Board members will be selected by a committee that includes the police commissioner, the mayor, a representative of the city council, and representatives of the community at large.
· Board members will be representative of the demographic makeup of the community.

- The police officer and the citizen will have equal representation.
- Hearings on complaints will take place within 90 days of the complaint.
- The results of the hearing will be made available to the public.

10. Make community policing skills essential for promotion.
> PREMISE: In order to be fit for a leadership position in the department, an officer must demonstrate proven skills in working with the community.

- Reinforce the department position that community policing constitutes crucial crime-prevention and peacekeeping activity.
- Abolish quota systems (formal and informal) for officer evaluation based on the number of arrests and citations.
- Require all officers to participate in ten hours of community-related activities each month.
- Offer incentives for officers to live in the communities they serve.

Afterword

AS THE TWIG IS BENT . . .

The single mission of reform is to provide our children with a legacy of peace and opportunity. We cannot expect of our law enforcement agencies what we do not demand of ourselves. We can't teach cooperation when our own hearts are hardened.

A final story.

It's Mother's Day, and I set aside my work on this book. As I often do, I take my two young kids and drive north to Vallejo to spend the afternoon with my mother. My mother is a beautiful, dignified woman in her seventies, as fully engaged in community life today as she was thirty years ago. It was my mother who nurtured my passion for justice when I was still a young boy; it was my mother who kept me on the straight and narrow.

When we arrive, my mother's modest house is packed with people coming and going, filling their plates with an impossible assortment of foods—turkey, fried chicken, ham, pasta, dressing, mashed potatoes, beans, greens, potato salad, rolls, cornbread, relishes, pies. No one ever goes hungry in my mother's home.

It is a mild, sunny day, and after lunch Mama and I decide to take a drive north to the orchards where we used to pick fruit for extra money when I was young. We leave the kids behind to play with their cousins, and start the twenty-minute ride north. I can never drive these roads without remembering the way Daddy's old pickup would gasp and crawl up the hills, burdened with the weight of our bodies.

We reach the fields—pretty as a picture, with tidy rows of trees and bushes all laid out like a patchwork quilt, getting ready to drop their bountiful fruit. As we drive along the narrow roads between the fields, Mama and I laugh and reminisce about the old days, stopping now and then to point to a familiar spot.

Suddenly there is a loud screech and a rising cloud of dust as a pickup truck comes barreling toward us on the road. It slams to a halt a few feet away, and a stocky white man, dressed in farmer's clothes and wearing an ugly scowl, races up to the car. Behind him, a woman in a tattered dress emerges, holding a naked baby. Her mouth is set in a thin line of disgust, and her eyes flash with indignation. The scene is vaguely surreal—something you might see in an old movie. Except it is happening now, to us.

"Who do you think you are, *nigger,* driving around here like you own the place?" the man demands.

"We're just leaving," I reply calmly, but he wants more. He's ready for a confrontation.

"I want to know what you think you're doing," he rasps.

I am painfully aware of how isolated we are, of how easily this situation could get out of control. I realize there is nothing I can tell the man; my credentials are meaningless here. My mother's goodness is meaningless.

"If you're concerned, call the police," I say.

"Get the hell out of here!" he screams.

I point out that he has us hedged in with his truck. "If you move, we'll go."

There is a long pause, which feels endless. A silent understanding passes between us. He's not going to move. He wants me to get out of my car and deal with him. We are frozen in that moment when anything is possible, when lives change forever.

Finally, still staring into his eyes, I shift my body slightly so he can see my Alameda County Police Athletic League T-shirt. Then he spins around and gets back into his truck. He screeches into reverse with an angry roar, moving just enough to allow us to edge past him.

My mother and I don't speak as we slowly drive down the long, narrow road. In my rearview mirror, I see the pickup on our tail, kicking up pebbles that spatter against the back window. I see the wide, observant eyes of the baby staring through the front windshield. I don't take a breath until we're back on the highway.

"I was so *scared*," my mother whispers. "So *scared*."

"You can't pay attention to ignorant folks like that," I tell her. "Put it out of your mind."

But the incident stays with me, smoldering. When you're black, you can never rise high enough to be safe from that kind of encounter. Add a rifle and a bottle of booze, and you're not around to talk about it anymore. My heart breaks with the notion that my son, such a smart, tough, and beautiful boy of ten, might grow up to feel this vulnerability. But my heart breaks, too, with the memory of that naked little baby's innocent eyes—recording everything, taking it all in.

Each of us, when we go home and look into the eyes of our children, must stand accountable for what we see there, for their eyes reflect only what is in our own.

"Just as the twig is bent, the tree's inclined," wrote Alexander Pope in his *Moral Essays*. Perhaps it is true that once the tree is inclined—toward bias, toward hatred—it cannot be unbent. But our children are young and delicate twigs, not yet bent. It's up to us to see that they grow into tall, straight trees whose roots go deep, and whose limbs stretch wide.

NOTES

CHAPTER 1: **A Man Who Cried**

Robert Davis:
United States District Court, Northern District of California.
Robert Davis and Jessica Davis v. *City of San Leandro*

Depositions:
Robert Davis—April 21, 1989
Jessica Davis—November 30, 1989
Officer Kenneth Marlin—November 22, 1989
Officer Diana Poor—November 22, 1989

CHAPTER 2: **Blacks and Cops in Conflict**

Christopher, et al. "Report of the Independent Commission on the
   Los Angeles Police Department." Los Angeles: Brixton Press, 1991.

St. Clair Commission. "Report of the Boston Police Department Management Review Committee." January 14, 1992.

"The Report of the Mollen Commission on the New York City Police Department." July 1994.

Amnesty International, Human Rights Watch. "Shielded from Justice." Reports on police misconduct, civil liability, policy, citizen review, and monies paid in civil suits in Atlanta, Boston, Chicago, Detroit, Indianapolis, Los Angeles, Minneapolis, New Orleans, New York, Philadelphia, Portland, Providence, San Francisco, and Washington, D.C., June 1998.

Wright, Jonathan. "Human Rights Group Says Police Brutality Rampant in United States." Reuters, July 7, 1998.

Amnesty International. "Police Brutality Widespread Problem in New York City." *Amnesty News*, June 27, 1996.

Pate, Anthony M., Fridell, Lorie A., and Hamilton, Edwin E. *Police Use of Force: Official Reports, Citizen Complaints, and Legal Consequences.* Washington, D.C.: Police Foundation, 1993.

Skolnick, Jerome H., and Fyfe, James J. *Above the Law: Police and the Excessive Use of Force.* New York: Free Press, 1993.

Sontag, Deborah, and Barry, Dan. "The Price of Brutality: Police Complaints Settled, Rarely Resolved." *The New York Times*, September 17, 1997.

Office of Congressman John Conyers (14th District, Michigan). "Conyers Fights Legislation that Would Reduce Damage Awards for Police Brutality Victims." Press Release, re: "The Law Enforcement Officers Civil Liberty Act," December 15, 1995.

CHAPTER 3: **The Measure of a Man**

Melvin Black:

Burris, John L., Special Investigator. "Report of the Independent Investigation into the Fatal Shooting of Melvin Black by Oakland Police Officers." September 12, 1979.

"Release of Burris Report Asked." *Oakland Tribune*, September 26, 1979.

Payton, Brenda. "Cops Faulted in Youth's Death." *San Francisco Examiner*, September 15, 1979.

CHAPTER 4: **What Children See**

Darrell Hampton:

Interviews by Burris, John, and Whitney, Catherine, on August 4, 1998.

Fernandez, Elizabeth. "Oakland Cop's History of Abuse." *San Francisco Examiner*, November 6, 1990.

Darrel K. Hampton v. *City of Oakland, et al.* Investigative packet, August 4, 1993.

CHAPTER 5: **The Fox in the Henhouse**

Amnesty International, Human Rights Watch. "Shielded from Justice." Reports on police misconduct, civil liability, policy, citizen review, and monies paid in civil suits in Atlanta, Boston, Chicago, Detroit, Indianapolis, Los Angeles, Minneapolis, New Orleans, New York, Philadelphia, Portland, Providence, San Francisco, and Washington, D.C., June, 1998.

Bowden, Mark, et al. "Policing the Police: A Special Investigative Report." *Philadelphia Inquirer*, November 19, 1995.

American Civil Liberties Union of Northern California. "Failing the Test: Oakland's Police Complaint Process in Crisis." December 10, 1996.

———. "LAPD Complaint Process Still a Problem Five Years After Christopher Commission." July, 1996.

New York Civil Liberties Union. "A Fourth-Anniversary Overview of the Civilian Complaint Review Board: July 5, 1993–July 5, 1997." NYCLU, 1997.

American Civil Liberties Union, New York. "Police Abuse and Civilian Oversight." 1990.

Barry, Dan. "Independent Agency Fails to Police the Police, Critics Charge." *The New York Times*, September 15, 1997.

Smith, Chris. "The Police Police" *New York* magazine, September 22, 1997.

Kramer, Michael. "When Cops Go Bad." *Time* magazine, December 15, 1997.

Wilkes, Jr., Donald E. "Lawless Law Enforcement." Athens Human Rights Festival, May 1996.

Bricking, Tanya. "Civilian Oversight Gaining Popularity." *Cincinnati Enquirer*, February 11, 1998.

Werner Perez, Douglas. *Common Sense About Police Review*. Philadelphia: Temple University Press, 1994.

Bertha Ketter:
Bertha M. Ketter v. *City of Oakland, et al.* Investigative package, September 28, 1994.
Collins, Doug. "Freedom of Information? See You in Court." *Washington Free Press*, July/August, 1997.
Brenner, Marie. "Incident in the 70th Precinct." *Vanity Fair*, December 1997.
Fried, Joseph P. "Louima Sues, Asserting a Blue Wall of Silence." *The New York Times*, August 7, 1998.

CHAPTER 6: **Walking While Black**

Doug Stevens:
Interviews by Burris, John, and Whitney, Paul, on August 4, 1998.
Douglas Leon Stevens v. *City of Oakland, et al.* Investigative package, September 14, 1990.
Connelly, Brian. "The Death of Jonny Gammage." *Focus* magazine, 1995.
Herszenhorn, David M. "Inquiry Opened Into Shooting of 3 Black Men by New Jersey State Troopers." *The New York Times*, May 12, 1998.
Kifner, John, and Herszenhorn, David M. "Racial Profiling at Crux of Inquiry Into Shooting by Troopers." *The New York Times*, May 8, 1998.
Robinson, Bryan. "The Malice Green Case: No Justice, False Peace." Court TV Online, March 4, 1998.

Baraka Hull:
Interviews by Burris, John, and Whitney, Paul, on August 6, 1998.
United States District Court, Northern District of California. *Glenn Louis Hull, Brenda Curry, et al.* v. *City of Oakland and Officer Gil Tournour*. Coroner's Report, Sheriff's Department of Alameda County, for Baraka Patrick Hull, July 30, 1993.

CHAPTER 7: **The Continuum**

Oakland Police Department. *Training Bulletin*.
Los Angeles Police Department. *Training Bulletin*.

"Cops Can Use Pepper Spray." *San Francisco Examiner*, July 28, 1994.

Van Blaricom, D. P. "Excessive Force: What Is It and What Can Be Done About It?" *Law Enforcement News*, January 15, 1998.

American Civil Liberties Report. "Your Rights in an Encounter with the Police."

Nicodemus, Charles. "Asphyxiation in Chicago." *Chicago Sun-Times*, November 27, 1996.

Martin Trahan:

Interviews by Burris, John, and Whitney, Paul, on August 7, 1998.

Martinez, Don. "Cops Accused in Beating Death." *San Francisco Examiner*, August 4, 1989.

United States District Court, Northern District of California.

Mary Ellen Trahan, et al. v. *City of Oakland, et al.*

Depositions:

Mary Ellen Trahan—December 18, 1990

Khalylah M. Trahan—December 16, 1990

Martin Trahan, Jr.—December 17, 1991

Charles Vaughn:

De Santis, John. "Lawsuit Planned in Police Killing." *Monterey County Herald*, November 7, 1998

CHAPTER 8: **The Black Sea**

United States District Court, Northern District of California. *Scott Patterson, et al.* v. *City of Oakland, et al.* Investigative packet, January 15, 1996.

Depositions:

Kelvin Franklin—December 2, 1996

Patrick J. Simon—November 1, 1994

Didese Simpson—April 26, 1996

Marcus McDade—April 19, 1996

Chester Meadows—May 9, 1996

Anthony Knuckles—May 9, 1996

Diallobe Johnson—January 23, 1996

Kedar Ellis—February 16, 1996

Donald Breazell—January 26, 1996

John G. Peters, Jr.—March 17, 1997

Officer Michael Hallinan—May 6, 1996

Reserve Officer Dean Miller—February 20, 1996

Chief Michael Meyers—January 3, 1996

Slater, Dashka. "The Battle for the Lake." *East Bay Express,* June 17, 1994.

Williams, Diana M. "Festival Ends in Violence." *Oakland Tribune,* June 6, 1994.

Interviews by Burris, John, and Whitney, Paul, on August 4–5, 1998.

Frisby, Mister Mann. "Million Youth March Preps for Big Apple." New York *Daily News,* August 31, 1998.

"New York Top Cop Defends March Strategy." Associated Press, September 19, 1998.

CHAPTER 9: **Ain't I a Woman?**

Mahoney, Brett. "Jaywalker Says Police Used Excessive Force in Arrest." *Oakland Tribune,* October 17, 1991.

Jones, Will. "Suit for Brutality Filed for Jaywalking Arrest." *Oakland Tribune,* April 15, 1992.

Municipal Court, State of California. *People of the State of California* v. *Marguerite Martin.* Reporter's transcript of jury trial.

United States District Court, Northern District of California. *Marguerite Martin and Joyce Sept* v. *City of Oakland and Officer Inga Winkle.* Legal investigative package, April 14, 1992.

Interviews by Burris, John, and Whitney, Paul, on August 3, 1998.

CHAPTER 10: **A Failure to Communicate**

Martinez, Don. "Oakland Rapper Files Claim Against 2 Cops." *Oakland Tribune,* November 13, 1991.

United States District Court, Northern District of California. *Tupac Amaru Shakur* v. *City of Oakland, et al.*

Deposition:
Tupac Shakur—May 9, 1994

CHAPTER 11: **Skin So Blue**

Cheevers, Jack. "Oakland Cop Files Claim Over Assault by Colleagues." *Oakland Tribune,* December 6, 1988.

Stewart, Pearl. "The Cop Who Could Be King." *East Bay Express,* May 8, 1992.

United States District Court, Northern District of California. *Derrick D. Norfleet* v. *City of Oakland, et al.*

Depositions:
Derrick D. Norfleet—September 29, 1989
Michael Cefalu—February 19, 1991
Bernard Thurman—February 20, 1990

Interviews by Burris, John, and Whitney, Paul, on August 8, 1998.
Beals, Gregory, and Bai, Matt. "The Thin Blue Line." *Newsweek* magazine, September 1, 1997.
Zuckoff, Mitchell, and O'Neill, Gerard. " 'Testilying' Reporting Plan Set Up—Questionable Police Cases Will be Referred to Commissioner, DA." *Boston Globe,* December 27, 1997.
Coroner's report—Martin Trahan.
Barrett, Devlin. "Hugs for Louima Cop at Scandal Precinct." *New York Post,* December 13, 1997.

CHAPTER 12: **The Partnership**

Reports:
Office of Community-oriented Policing (COPS)
Community Policing Consortium
U.S. Department of Justice
Claim against the City of Oakland, CA: *Barbara J. Dean* v. *Police Chief George Hart and Officer Joseph Sweeney.* Investigative package, September 5, 1990.
United States District Court, District of Northern California. *Barbara J. Dean and Shonda Jones* v. *City of Oakland, et al.* Investigative package, December 16, 1991.
Interviews by Burris, John, and Whitney, Paul, on August 11, 1998.

CHAPTER 13: **The Making of a Good Cop**

Christopher, et al. "Report of the Independent Commission on the Los Angeles Police Department." Los Angeles: Brixton Press, 1991.

Index

Acorn Community Center, 44, 45, 58
Amnesty International, 69, 70
Antislavery Society, 81
Arbitration, 69. *See also* Police departments: practices
Aristotle, 203
Autobiography of Miss Jane Pittman, The, 41

Baird, Jeff, 182
Batons, 112–113
Black, Melvin, 32–37, 100
Black Panther Party, 30, 31
Blue vs. Black, 2

"Blue wall." *See* Code of silence
Bostic, Michael, 18
Boston Police Department, 19
Boyovich, Alexander, 48, 51, 160
Brewer, Abner, 117, 118
Briseno, Ted, 181, 182
Brutality. *See* Police abuse; Police misconduct
Bulls, Larnell, 98

Camus, Albert, 169
Cefalu, Mike, 171, 172, 174, 177

Chemical sprays, 109–111, 133

Chicago: CAPS teams, 196–197

Police Department, 20, 23

Children: effects of violence on, 56–59

Chokeholds, 113–114, 118

Chon, Tom, 171, 172

Christopher Commission, 17–18, 76, 163, 210

Citizen advisory boards, 197

Citizen complaints, 218, 219

Civilian review boards, 63, 69–70, 221–222

problems of, 74–77

Civil rights cases, 62, 162, 220

Civil-rights law, 37, 131

Code of silence, 38, 177–180, 181, 183

Collier, Steven, 131

Communication, 163–164, 166–167, 195, 215, 216

Community policing, 187–202, 217, 222

effectiveness of, 190, 195, 196–198, 199, 202

purposes of, 187, 189, 200–201

tactics of, 191–192

Community Policing Consortium, 198

Complaint Review Board (N.Y.C.), 69, 70

Continuum of force, 107, 108, 120

Conyers, John, Jr., 25

Copwatch, 78

Crowd control, 131–132, 138–139

Curry, Brenda, 100, 102, 103-104

Daley, Richard, 30

Darden, Christopher, 203

Dateline NBC, 65

Davis, Robert, 5–13, 108, 112

Davis, Ron, 170, 171, 172, 173

Davis, V. J., 117

Deadly force. *See* Weapons

Dean, Barbara, 192–196

Detroit, Michigan, Police Department, 23

Diallo, Amadou, 103

District attorney's office, 97–98

Drummond, William, 155

DWB. *See* Stereotyping

Ellis, Kedar, 124, 125, 127–129

Ellison, Ralph, 123

El Paso Police Department, 197–198

Emerson, Ralph Waldo, 107

Equal Employment Opportunity Commission, 71

Flashlights, 112–113
Foley, Hasha, 85, 88, 90
Fortune, Bobby, 99–100
Fuhrman, Mark, 40, 203

Gaines, Ernest J., 41
Gammage, Jonny, 96
Gates, Daryl, 18
Green, Malice, 98
Grimes, Milton, 38
Giuliani, Rudy, 73

Hall, Dwayne, 82, 83, 87, 89,
     90
Hampton, Darrell, 43–57, 58-
     59, 64, 108, 190
Hampton, Fred, 30–31
Harris, Ted, 131
Hearing process, 71. *See also*
     Police
Hoffman, John, 70
Hong, Paul, 148
Hull, Baraka, 100–104
Human Rights Watch, 19, 22

Indianapolis, Ind., 24
Internal Affairs Divisions:
     investigations by, 63–65,
     68–69, 175. *See also*
     Police department

Jaywalking, 164, 165
Jefferson, Thomas, 187
Johnson, Diallobe, 130

Ketter, Bertha, 66–68
King, Martin Luther, Jr., 27,
     31
King, Rodney, 16, 17, 99
     case, 38, 92, 97, 112, 181,
     211
Knuckles, Anthony, 123, 130,
     133–134
Kumin, Matthew, 131
Kunstler, William, 182

Latino Officers' Association,
     71–72
Lawbreaking, 16–17
Law Enforcement Officers'
     Civil Liberty Act, 24–25
Lerner, Max, 61
Lewis, T. K., 66, 67
Liller, Tracy, 98
Lipset, Hal, 33
Los Angeles, California, riots,
     16
Los Angeles Police Department
     (LAPD), 18, 22, 39
     training, 18
Louima, Abner, 73, 186

McDade, Marcus, 130
McDowell, Willie, 117, 118,
     119
Malcolm X, 15
Martin, Marguerite, 142–
     148, 150, 155–156
Media: attitudes, 2, 39, 188
Metcalfe Commission, 20, 30

Meyerson, James I., 78
Million Youth March, 138
Mollen Commission, 18, 75, 182
Moorhead, Carlos, 24, 25
Muhammad, Khalid Abdul, 138
Mulligan, Robert A., 184

New Orleans Police Department, 72
New York Police Department (NYPD), 18, 22, 68, 69–70, 185–186, 205
Norfleet, Derrick, 169–177, 178, 198–202
Nutter, Michael, 69

Oakland, California, 42–43, 82, 123-124
  Police Department, 23, 32, 47, 72, 175, 199, 210
Orozco, Ricardo, 83, 84-87, 89

Patterson, Scott, 130
Perot, H. Ross, 40
Philadelphia Inquirer, 69
Philadelphia Police Department, 18–19, 64–65, 68-69
Pittsburgh Police Department, 96

Police:
  abuse, 16, 19–20, 40, 73–74, 84–89, 117, 120, 179
  accountability, 78–79
  attitudes, 142, 208–212
  attitudes toward, 159–163
  conflicts with, 16–17
  corruption, 182–186
  and costs of abuse, 21–25, 57–58, 90, 99–100
  importance of leadership to, 38, 218
  misconduct, 3, 6, 18–19, 20–21, 25, 62–63, 66–68, 71, 77, 78–79, 96, 101–102, 107, 162–163, 220–221
  showing respect for, 157
  training, 38, 107–111, 112, 113, 120–121, 137–139, 145–146, 147, 155–159, 163–167, 212, 215–217, 220
  unions, 19
Police Athletic League, 196
Police Commission:
  Los Angeles, 76
  San Francisco, 76, 111
Police department: blueprint for reform, 214–222
  investigations, 63–65, 68–69, 102
  penalty system, 71–72

policies, 71, 106, 112, 131–
    133, 134, 147, 191
practices, 62, 102–103, 106,
    107–111, 218
promoting effectiveness of,
    218–222
recruitment standards, 205–
    207, 214–215
Pope, Alexander, 226
Portland, Oregon, 78
Press. *See* Media

Racial prejudice, 208–211
Reno, Janet, 20
Review boards, 63, 69–70,
    221–222
    problems of, 74–77
Roache, Francis, 19
Rogue cops, 72–74, 150–153,
    203. *See also* Police abuse;
    Police misconduct
Roth, Kenneth, 20
Rowan, Carl T., 213
Russo, Monica, 86

Safir, Howard, 73, 138
San Francisco, California,
    Police Department, 23, 76–
    78
San Francisco Examiner, 77
Seals, Ray, 96
Seattle Police Department, 70
Sept, Joyce, 150–154
Shakur, Tupac, 159–160

Shootings, 102–103
Simon, Patrick, 130, 135–137
Simpson, O. J., murder case,
    39–40
Stenson, Andre, 98
Stereotyping, 16, 95–96, 105–
    106, 210–211
Stevens, Doug, 81–94, 108
Stillwell, Willard, 110–111
Street Crime Unit (N.Y.C.), 103
Stun guns, 7, 10, 112

Tasers, 7, 10
Thomas, Betty, 109, 110
Thompson, Charles, 98
Thurman, Bernard, 171, 172
Tournour, Gildo, 101, 102–
    103
Trahan, Martin, 114–121, 185
Trahan, Mary, 114, 117
Truth, Sojourner, 141
Twain, Mark, 5

U.S. Justice Department, 20

Vaughn, Charles, 121–122
Verbal Judo. *See*
    Communication

Walker, Sam, 76
Wallace, William, 118
Washington, D.C., Police
    Department, 22–23
Weapons, 111–114

Williams, Aaron, 111
Williams, Officer, 66, 67
Wilson, Lionel, 33
Winkle, Inga, 143–153, 155
Woods, Victor, 49

Yoakum, Charlie, 109–110
Yoell, Michael, 46, 47–48, 49–
  50, 51, 53, 56, 58, 61, 64

Ziomek, Katzuko, 149–150